DON'T BREAK THE BANK: A STUDENT'S GUIDE TO MANAGING MONEY
2012

About Peterson's Publishing

Peterson's Publishing provides the accurate, dependable, high-quality education content and guidance you need to succeed. No matter where you are on your academic or professional path, you can rely on Peterson's print and digital publications for the most up-to-date education exploration data, expert test-prep tools, and top-notch career success resources—everything you need to achieve your goals.

For more information, contact Peterson's, 2000 Lenox Drive, Lawrenceville, NJ 08648;

800-338-3282 Ext. 54229; or find us online at www.petersonspublishing.com.

Bernadette Webster, Managing Editor; Jill C. Schwartz, Editor; Ray Golaszewski, Publishing Operations Manager; Tim Conboy, eBook Production Associate; Bobbi Dempsey, Author; Ovetta Sampson, Contributing Writer/Researcher, John Dempsey, Contributing Researcher

ISBN-13: 978-0-7689-3647-6

ISBN-10: 0-7689-3647-0

First Edition

Certified Chain of Custody

60% Certified Fiber Sourcing and
40% Post-Consumer Recycled

www.sfiprogram.org

*This label applies to the text stock.

Sustainability—Its Importance to Peterson's Publishing

What does sustainability mean to Peterson's Publishing? As a leading publisher, we are aware that out business has a direct impact on vital resources—most especially the trees that are used to make out books. Peterson's Publishing is proud that its products are certified to the Sustainable Forestry Initiative (SFI) chain-of-custody standard and that all of its books are printed on paper that is 40 percent post-consumer waste using vegetable-based ink.

Being a part of the Sustainable Forestry Initiative (SFI) means that all of out vendors—from paper suppliers to printers—have undergone rigorous audits to demonstrate that they are maintaining a sustainable environment.

Peterson's Publishing continuously strives to find new ways to incorporate sustainability throughout all aspects of its business.

Check out the *Don't Break the Bank* mobile app to help you better plan, save, and spend!

Available in iTunes, Android & GooglePlay

A LETTER TO STUDENTS

Dear Student:

There are lots of old sayings about money: that it makes the world go around, that it doesn't buy happiness, and even that it's the root of all evil. Whether or not you believe any of those, it's hard to deny that money will play an important role in your life. You need money to pay for your basic living needs—like food and shelter—and to buy the fun things—like clothing and electronics.

If you are like most young adults, your parents took care of money issues for most of your life up until this point. You may have gotten an allowance and perhaps have earned some extra money babysitting or mowing lawns, but for the most part, your parents probably handled your expenses and earned most of the household income.

But you are quickly approaching (or have already reached) the point where you need to know more about money. You may be getting ready to apply for a job, or perhaps you have a cell phone bill or other expenses to pay. And you might be starting to worry about how to save or invest some of the money you earn.

Don't Break the Bank: A Student's Guide to Managing Money can help you learn the basics about earning, saving, budgeting, and investing your money. This book is divided in specific parts on major money topics: what money is, how to earn it, why it's important to save it, and how to invest it. You will also learn tips on how to create and stick to a budget, and you'll find out why good credit is so important. The habits and decisions you make right now can affect your finances for a long time, so we want to help you get the best possible start.

Bottom line: you'll learn how to spend, save, and manage your money in a smart way—and plan a budget that splurges so you can have fun without, well, breaking the bank.

We hope you will find this publication useful in helping you learn how to manage your own finances. If you have feedback on *Don't Break the Bank*, please contact us at: custsvc@petersons.com

Sincerely,

Peterson's Editorial Staff

10 Steps to Increase Your Financial Fitness

1. Be honest about where you are.

It's human nature to avoid pain, but denying a problem will only make it worse. Statistics show that more than one third of Americans purposely avoid thinking about their damaged financial lives. Until we get honest with ourselves, we are unlikely to improve our financial health. To become financially fit, it's important to know things like:

Your credit score—What is it? What does it mean? How do you get it?

How much you owe and to whom?—Are you paying rent, insurance, everyday expenses?

How much do you have in savings?—Are you spending every cent you have? How much should you be saving?

How much have you saved for retirement? When should you start a retirement account?

Where are your investments held? How they are allocated?

2. Know where you want to be.

Changing habits can be tough. To stay motivated, keep your eyes on the prize. What would a healthy financial life do for you? How would it make you feel? What would you have? Where would you go? Identify your goals around your career, education, retirement someday, travel, health, and family. Where do you want to be in five years? In ten years? The more specifically you identify what you want, the more energy you will unleash to get yourself there.

3. Beware of your thoughts.

Are you an over-spender? Do you neglect saving? If you answered "yes," you are an average American. Perhaps that helps explain why 80 percent of Americans say money is the Number 1 source of stress in their lives. To change bad habits, it is often essential to identify the beliefs that underlie them. Our financial behaviors make sense when we understand our beliefs about money. These beliefs, called money scripts, are typically outside our conscious awareness, but they drive all our financial behaviors. Some problematic money scripts include the following: "More money or more things will make me happier," and "I can never have what I want, so I might as well get what I can when I can." When we base our financial lives on erroneous or incomplete beliefs, we set ourselves up for failure.

4. Forgive yourself.

Our feelings and beliefs about money don't develop in a vacuum. We are taught them or we arrive at them when trying to make sense of confusing situations. As children, we are prone to making incomplete conclusions. For example, if our family is rich and unhappy, we may conclude that money led to our unhappiness, when the discontentment could be better explained by other issues. As adults, we rarely return to our past, identify our money scripts, examine them, or change them. As a result, their control over our financial lives can be insidious. So, regardless of your current financial situation, have compassion for yourself. Most likely, your behavior toward money is a result of where you came from. The good news is, the more you know about money management the more you are empowered to change.

5. Commit to change (if you are ready).

Change takes time, energy, and effort. To change, we must believe it is important to do so. To examine whether you're ready to change, write down the pros and cons. What are the pros of staying where you are, such as continuing to buy what you want, travel, or not have to think about finances (at least for a while)? What are the cons of continuing to do what you are doing, such as spending your money on entertainment instead of being able to pay your car insurance? Or getting into credit card debt so the $40 shirt you bought becomes an $80 shirt due to interest? You will commit to change only when your list of benefits outweighs your list of reasons to stay right where you are. Even if you are not ready to transform your financial life, consider taking Step 6 anyway. When you are ready to commit to improving your financial fitness, you are well on your way.

6. Apply some "financial first aid."

In health care, first aid is meant to prevent further harm and promote recovery. If someone is bleeding, first aid may involve applying pressure to the wound. Instead of losing blood, over-spenders bleed money, and much of it is borrowed. Financial first aid involves putting a stop to overspending and oftentimes halting the use of credit cards. Shop with cash to help avoid impulse buying. It might seem like a small action, but it can be a giant leap toward financial fitness. Studies show we spend 30 percent less when we pay with cash. So take action now to stop the bleeding.

7. Make a plan.

To stay on top of our finances, we need a plan for spending, saving, and giving. A spending plan allows for meeting financial obligations and needs, while allowing for saving and giving. Your plan may include reducing spending in some areas, while setting aside more money in others. Once your plan is in place, track it. You may find some checking and budgeting software helpful. You may choose to save 10–30 percent of your income. You may choose to set up direct deposits to your savings account to ensure you pay yourself first.

8. Take action.

It takes about 30 days of practice before a new behavior becomes a habit. With a plan in place, you can begin tracking your spending, finding ways to save money, and spending money on the things that matter most. Living a life in which your financial behaviors match your values and goals feels good. Being conscious and purposeful about spending can help us appreciate and enjoy life more.

9. Expect challenges.

It is important to know that you may slip back into old habits. For the most important changes, relapse is common and should be expected. The important thing is to not beat yourself up about it. Get back on track as soon as possible. See bumps along the way as learning experiences.

10. Ask for help.

The journey to financial health can be long. There will be setbacks along the way. If you find yourself repeating mistakes or having trouble following through on your plan, seek the help of a parent or another trusted adult.

Source: Dr. Brad Klontz, on behalf of H&R Block Dollars and Sense http://www.hrbds.com

TABLE OF CONTENTS

PART 1
MONEY, MONEY, MONEY...

You probably know a lot about money. You know how much you need to buy what you really want. And, of course, you know how tough it can sometimes be to get your hands on money. But how much do you know about money itself—as in, actual currency? You've probably never given it much thought, but there are lots of interesting things to learn about paper currency and coins. You'll find out what the words and symbols mean, how inflation affects your money, and what it's like to use money in other parts of the world.

CHAPTER 1
ALL ABOUT MONEY

There's no denying that money plays an important role in our lives. Virtually everything we do involves money in some way. Unless you are a mystical guitar player who lives off magic beans and the goodwill of strangers, you will need money to survive. Still, right now, as a teenager, your life probably resembles that mystical guitar player's existence. If you need something to eat, it magically appears on the dinner table. If you need something to wear, you're instantly transported to the mall. But pretty soon this idyllic life will disappear as mom and dad will no longer foot the bill for all your needs and wants. Sooner than you think, if you want to enjoy the comforts of life, you'll have to earn, save, and possess money. This book is designed to help you do just that. You're never too young to learn about money and how to manage it.

Yes, it sounds boring, but before you close your eyes in disgust, just visualize that new MacBook, or iPod, or red pair of Toms that you've been dreaming about. All these things cost money, and if you do not know how to handle it, well, they will remain wishes instead of possessions. You don't want to be the only one in your college dorm room who actually has to eat Ramen noodles to survive instead of consuming them as part of your hipster quotient, do you? If not, buckle up for a quick and dirty lesson about a commodity that began as beef and evolved into actual metal coins—yes, we're talking about MONEY!

THE ABBREVIATED AND COMPLETELY COOL HISTORY OF MONEY

9000 B.C.—Some guy sees fire for the first time and offers a cow in exchange for a piece of the hot light. Or maybe not! But the oldest form of money was, yep, you guessed it, a cow.

Cows were used to exchange value for everything from brides to bags until about 2000 B.C., when man melded metal into the shape of cows and used them as the first form of non-living money.

1690: Ever the progressive folk, the people of The Massachusetts Bay Colony, one of America's 13 original colonies, issue the first paper money to cover costs of military expeditions. The practice of issuing paper bills spreads to the other colonies.

1730: Ben Franklin's Philadelphia printing company prints Colonial Bills, which feature nature prints—raised impressions created from casts of real leaves. This doesn't just look pretty; it actually is a clever way to make it harder to make counterfeit bills.

1785: Congress recognizes the dollar as the official paper currency of the United States.

1792: The Coinage Act of 1792 creates the U.S. Mint, establishes a federal money system, and sets the denominations for U.S. coins.

1861: The federal government first circulates paper money to help finance the Civil War. The bills are known as "greenbacks" because of their color.

1865: The Secret Service is created to protect—nope, not the President—but the nation's money against counterfeiting. Ironically, the law creating the Secret Service was on President Lincoln's desk the day he went to a certain theater and never came home. Bonus: When did Congress authorize the Secret Service to protect the President and other high-ranking American leaders?

1913: The Federal Reserve Act establishes a national banking system.

2000: The U.S. Treasury introduce the redesigned $5 and $10 bills in an anti-counterfeiting effort. The new $5 and $10 bills featured oversized and a bit off-centered pictures of Abraham Lincoln and Alexander Hamilton. Other measures to counter counterfeiting includes watermarks that can be seen under a light, security threads that glow when exposed to ultraviolet light, and tiny printing that's visible with the help of a magnifying glass. The $100, $50, and $20 bill underwent similar makeovers in 1996, 1997, and 1998, respectively.

2003: As the U.S. Secret Service is integrated into the new U.S. Department of Homeland Security, protecting the security of the dollar against counterfeiting joins other homeland security efforts.

2004: The $50 bill is redesigned and issued on September 28, 2004. Similar to the redesigned $20 bill, the redesigned $50 bill features historical symbols of Americana (a waving American flag and a small metallic silver-blue star).

2010: The new design of the $100 bill is presented by officials from the U.S. Department of the Treasury, the Federal Reserve Board, and the U.S. Secret Service on April 21. Complete with advanced technology to combat counterfeiting, the new design for the $100 note retains the traditional look of U.S. currency. For more information, see "The $100 Bill" later in this chapter.

How Does Money Get Printed?

Money is printed in Fort Worth, Texas and Washington D.C., by the Bureau of Engraving and Printing, which is a division of the U.S. Department of the Treasury.

Production facts from the Bureau of Engraving and Printing:

- Approximately 23.5 million notes per day, with a face value of approximately $453 million, were produced in 2011.
- Approximately 5.8 billion notes at an average cost of 9.1 cents per note were delivered in 2011.
- Ninety-five percent of the notes printed each year are used to replace notes already in, or taken out, of circulation.
- Approximately 8.5 tons of ink used each day at the Bureau of Engraving and Printing's Fort Worth and Washington, D.C., facilities during Fiscal Year 2011.

WHEN MONEY GOES BAD...

Money never goes bad, seriously. Even money that has been damaged in major ways such as in a fire or flood or even being buried can still be redeemed for face value. The Treasury calls this "mutilated money," and you can send your damaged money to them, and they will try to salvage enough of it to indentify how much was there and then redeem it for the face value. Check it out: http://www.moneyfactory.gov/uscurrency/damagedcurrency.html. If you have currency that has just been slightly torn or otherwise damaged in a minor way, you can take it to a bank to be redeemed.

THE LIFESPAN OF A BILL

New money is constantly being printed, partly because older bills need to be replaced. The average lifespan of a bill ranges from 4.7 years for a $1 bill to 21.6 years for a $100 bill, according to the U.S. Department of the Treasury. Larger bills tend to last longer because people tend to hold on to them longer and only use them for larger purchases or special occasions. Since they aren't handled as often, they don't wear out as quickly as smaller bills.

> The largest bill being printed by the Department of the Treasury today is the $100 bill. The government previously printed bills in denominations of $500; $1,000; $5,000, and $10,000, but stopped printing these in 1945. These bills are still considered legal tender, though, so you could spend them—if you were lucky enough to get your hands on one.

A LOOK AT EACH BILL*

THE $100 BILL

The first $100 U.S. notes were issued by the federal government in 1862 and featured an image of an eagle.

Today, the front of the $100 bill features Benjamin Franklin. The back of the $100 bill shows Independence Hall in Philadelphia. The hall is an important part of U.S. history because it was where the Declaration of Independence was signed and the Constitution of the United States was drafted. It is often called the birthplace of our nation.

*[Images courtesy of the Bureau of Engraving and Printing.]

THE $50 BILL

The front of the $50 bill shows Ulysses Grant, the eighteenth president of the United States. The back shows the U.S. Capitol. Like several of the other bills, the $50 bill has been updated a few times recently for security purposes.

The use of the National Motto *In God We Trust* on all currency has been required by law since 1955. It first appeared on U.S. coins in 1864, on paper money with $1 Silver Certificates in 1957, and on Federal Reserve Notes starting with the 1963 Series.

THE $20 BILL

The $20 bill shows Andrew Jackson, the seventh U.S. president, on the front and the White House on the back.

THE $10 BILL

The $10 Bill shows Alexander Hamilton (first Secretary of the Treasury) on the front and the U.S. Treasury Building on the back.

Look closely, and you'll see that there is a car pictured on the back. Contrary to popular belief, it is not a Model "T" Ford. It is just a fictional car created by the designer of the bill. The $10 Bill has been updated several times in recent years with added security features.

THE $5 BILL

The $5 bill shows Abraham Lincoln, the sixteenth president of the United States, on the front and the Lincoln Memorial on the back.

The $5 bill has been updated a couple of times since the mid-1990s to add more security features.

THE $2 BILL

The $2 bill shows Thomas Jefferson, the third U.S. president, on the front. The Declaration of Independence is on the back.

THE $1 BILL

  The first $1 Federal Reserve Notes were issued in 1963, and the design with George Washington on the front and the Great Seal on the back has remained the same since then.

MAJOR U.S. COINS

U.S. coins are produced by the United States Mint, which has six locations across the country. Current facilities include the headquarters in Washington, D.C.; production facilities in Philadelphia, Pennsylvania; West Point, New York; Denver, Colorado; and San Francisco, California; and the United States Bullion Depository at Fort Knox, Kentucky.

PENNY

The penny features a picture of Abraham Lincoln on the front. The images on the back have changed over the years—the latest design shows a union shield with a scroll across it that says, "ONE CENT."

NICKEL

The nickel shows Thomas Jefferson on the front and Monticello (Jefferson's estate in Virginia) on the back.

DIME

The dime is the smallest and thinnest of the coins in use today. The front shows Franklin Roosevelt, and the back shows a design with a torch, an olive branch, and an oak branch.

QUARTER

The quarter (short for the quarter-dollar) features George Washington on the front. The design on the back has featured lots of different images in recent years.

From 1999 to 2008, the U.S. Mint conducted the 50 State Quarters program, where special quarters were released, one for each state, in the order in which the states joined the Union. Starting in 2010, the Mint began releasing a series of 56 quarters with designs of national parks and other important national sites as part of the America the Beautiful Quarters program.

This is the reverse side of the Yellowstone National Park version of the quarter (issued as part of the America the Beautiful Quarters program).

HALF-DOLLAR

The half-dollar features John F. Kennedy on the front and a design based on the presidential seal on the back.

DOLLAR

Right now, there are two dollar coins being produced in the United States: the Presidential $1 Coin Series (started in 2007) and the Native American $1 Coin. Both types of dollar coins look golden in color, although there is no gold in the mixture of metals used to make these coins.

PRESIDENTIAL $1 COIN   NATIVE AMERICAN $1 COIN

MONEY AROUND THE WORLD

If you travel outside of the United States, take your dollars with you! You can exchange them for the local currency in the airport but, more often than not, folks will love to take your American money. You may also be able to exchange U.S. currency at a large U.S. bank or monetary exchange center in the U.S. airport before your flight departs.

If you don't want to haul bunches of cash with you overseas—if you carry more than $10,000 on you at a time you have to declare the amount to U.S. Immigration and Customs officers at the airport—then one solution is to buy traveler's checks. You can buy them here and then use them in other countries. The good thing about traveler's checks is they can be replaced if they are lost or stolen. Money lost, sadly, is money gone!

Another option, and one that is becoming increasingly popular these days, is a Prepaid Travel Card. This works just like an ATM/check card, but it offers the protection of traveler's checks. You can purchase a Visa® or MasterCard® travel card before you leave the United States and then use it at merchants or ATMs just like an ATM/check card. The beauty of such cards is that they are prepaid—so you know exactly how much money you have to spend—and they generally offer the security of replacement if stolen.

While overseas, you should be able to get cash from an ATM machine. But remember, you'll be getting cash in the LOCAL CURRENCY. This can present some problems, especially if the exchange rate is outrageous. For example, let's say you withdraw $500 from an ATM in India. With an exchange rate of $1 U.S. Dollar for every 55 Indian Rupees, you might have to buy another travel bag to fit the 27,500 Rupees you're going to get! Better to use check/debit cards, or U.S. money whenever possible, rather than be stuck with stacks of foreign currency and no way to unload them safely.

If you use a large bank that has an office/bank in the country you're visiting, you should have no problems getting cash in the right currency from the ATM. Otherwise, keep in mind that when you withdraw cash from an ATM, you'll probably be charged a service fee. Also, be sure to alert your U.S. bank BEFORE you travel, and let them know which countries you will be visiting. That way, if you do need to use an ATM, you won't be denied access to your account—without notification, there's a good chance your bank might think someone has stolen your card and is using it in another country.

GLOBAL MONEY MATH CHALLENGES

Let's practice some global money skills. You are traveling to some popular tourist spots around the world, and you need to figure out if you have enough money to buy the souvenir or other item you want. You will need to know the exchange rate—what the currency in one country is worth in the local currency of another country. We've provided the exchange rate (current when we wrote this chapter but no doubt different now). You need to determine if you can buy what you want. (*See below for the correct answers!*)

SCENARIO 1: YOUR SCHOOL BAND IS TOURING LONDON TODAY.

[Current exchange rate: 1 U.S. Dollar (USD) = 0.63 British Pounds or 1 GBP = 1.5635 USD]

After watching the changing of the Royal Guard, you spend some time staking out the neighborhood near Buckingham Palace but are disappointed that you don't spot a single royal. However, you do see a gold-plated miniature replica of Big Ben in a souvenir shop. It costs 11 British Pounds. You have $20. Can you afford it?

SCENARIO 2: THE FRENCH CLUB STOPS IN PARIS.

[Current exchange rate: 1 USD = 0.748 (Euro) or 1 EUR = 1.3365 USD]

You are strolling around the boulevards in Paris. While gazing at the Eiffel Tower, you nearly walk by a tiny boutique, but a colorful silk scarf in the window catches your eye. The scarf costs 45 Euro. You think about how much you budgeted for this trip, and you realize that after your expensive, but delicious dinner last night, you can only afford to spend a maximum of 50 U.S. dollars. Can you purchase the scarf?

SCENARIO 3: YOUR BEST FRIEND INVITES YOU ON TO GO ON THEIR FAMILY VACATION TO CANCUN, MEXICO!

[Current exchange rate: 1 USD = 13.5079 Mexican Pesos (MXN) or 1 MXN = 0.07403 USD]

You're in Cancun and are browsing the popular open air flea market in the center of town. You want to buy a leather belt that costs 300 pesos. You remember seeing a similar belt for $20 in a store back home. Will this belt cost you less than that one?

ANSWERS:

Scenario 1: The correct answer is YES, you can buy the souvenir.

11 GBP = 17.1983 U.S. dollars

Cheerio! You have enough money, with a little change to spare.

Scenario 2: The correct answer is NO.

45 Euro = 60.093 US dollars

You will have to say, "Je regrette je ne peux pas acheter l'écharpe. ("I regret I cannot buy the scarf.") You won't be able to buy the scarf, since you only can spend the equivalent of 37.4427 Euro.

Scenario 3: The correct answer is NO.

300 Pesos = 22.1707 US dollars

The belt costs more money than the one you saw in the store back home. But haggling is commonplace—and usually expected—in flea markets in Mexico, so you should be able to negotiate and get that belt for less than 20 U.S. dollars.

THE FUTURE OF MONEY IS NOW

In the 1990s, a renegade Stanford computer engineer and a few pals decided they wanted to disrupt what they deemed was the corrupt global banking system by offering an easier, frictionless, virtual currency system that allowed individuals from all over the world to exchange values without exorbitant costs. Peter Thiel's vision soon became PayPal, and while it didn't tear down the banking system, it certainly made it easier for millions to perform online money transactions. More significant than Paypal's attempt to change our money system is its effect upon innovation in the virtual currency world. PayPal was the grandfather to a whole host of virtual money arbiters that have ushered in an entirely new way of looking at money.

Thanks to giants like Paypal, eBay, and upstarts such as Dowalla and Square, these days, currency isn't just paper bills and coins. Now, lots of transactions occur outside of the physical world and are made up of invisible, virtual transactions that exchange value for both real and virtual products, goods, and services. Here are just a few:

BITCOIN: VIRTUAL CURRENCY FOR THE REAL WORLD

What if value could travel from one computer to another with the oversight of just a computer program and a few engineers and without the need for a central banking authority to monitor transactions or even the real identity of users to be revealed? Essentially, this is what's occurring with currently the only all-virtual currency in the world known as Bitcoin. Unlike Paypal, Square, or other online monetary transactions Bitcoins are not connected to a governmental banking system. A gang of computer engineers using open-source software keeps tabs on the amount of bitcoins in circulation, generates more bitcoins when necessary, and allows computers to exchange bitcoin values without worrying about intangibles such as trust or validity.

GAMER CURRENCY

Gamer currency is where you pay real money for items in a game or virtual world. You may also use it to buy a membership or access to play the game. Major gaming console systems use points as currency with which you can buy in-game items or the games themselves. For example, the Wii™ allows you to use Wii™ points to buy access to older Nintendo games that you can then play on your Wii™. Microsoft sells Xbox® points that you can use to buy things like extra songs for your Rock Band playlist.

Zynga, Inc., which makes several games that are played through Facebook®, sells credits that you can use to buy things like farm equipment in the FarmVille game.

> # TIP
> If you keep an eye out on deal-hunting sites like FatWallet.com, you can sometimes find coupon/ promo codes that you can use to buy gift cards at a discounted price.

For a game like World of Warcraft (an online multiplayer game), you buy cards that allow you access to play the game for a certain period of time— say, three months.

You can buy these "game currency" cards at major retail stores like Wal-Mart and Target. You can also usually just buy the points online directly from the company site or through the game's control panel. (However, by buying the prepaid cards at a retail store, you may be able to avoid having to enter your credit card information in your game account, which eliminates the security risk of having your information stolen or hacked.)

ITUNES CARDS

iTunes cards are gift cards that give you a certain amount of credit that you can use in the iTunes store for things like music and movie downloads. For people who like to download a lot of music or other content from iTunes, these cards can be worth their weight in gold.

GIFT CARDS AND/OR REBATE CARDS

> **TIP**
> Be sure to read the fine print on the back of your gift card. Some cards charge an "inactivity fee" if you don't use the card for a certain period of time.

You can find gift cards for just about every major store (including online-only stores or sites like eBay). This can be a good way to help stick to a budget. For example, if you want to make sure you don't spend more than $50 at Target this month, just buy a gift card for that amount and limit all your purchases to things you buy with that card. Once it doesn't have a balance, you've reached your limit. Even fast food places like Burger King and McDonald's have gift cards. If you've received gift cards that you won't use, you can go on a site like PlasticJungle.com, where you can sell your gift card or swap it for another gift card you want.

In addition, many companies that offer rebates or referral fees use pre-paid cards instead of money to award their prizes. These cards are usually accepted at all major retailers but be sure to read the fine print.

PART 2
WAYS TO EARN YOUR OWN CASH

Let's face it: Once you reach a certain age, getting an allowance can be embarrassing, and having to ask Mom and Dad for every dollar can be a real pain. Even worse, your parents may give you the third degree about what you're spending money on, and most likely, they'll feel you can do without the things you consider necessities. The bottom line: You need to start making your own money. Besides, it won't be long until you're supposed to be a self-sufficient adult buying your own food, clothes, and assorted other items, so this would be a good time to do a "practice run" of what it's like to support yourself—even though you're really only earning spending money. As bonus, this experience can help you get a glimpse into the working world and what type of job you might like— or one you might want to avoid.

CHAPTER 2
PART-TIME JOBS AND WAYS TO MAKE MONEY

Now that we've learned all about money's place in our society, it's time to turn this conversation personal. As we stated in Chapter 1, people need money to survive. Teens, it seems, are no exception. In 2012, your 25.6 million peers spent more than $208.7 billion. That's a lot of iPods, clothes, shoes, video games, and so on. Just where did they get all that money? Well, as you probably already know, some of that money came from parents. But increasingly, teens are becoming responsible for their own income, and that means getting a job. Believe it or not, even teens as young as 14 years old can legally work in the United States—with restrictions of course. By age 16, federal work rules are pretty much the same as they are for adults. Working has always been an option for adolescents who want to earn some dough. At least it's the best way to get the bling without getting arrested. Each year, American teens earn about $91 billion working summer and part-time jobs. Yes, we know that working isn't usually a lot of fun, but you do have a lot of different options, so you might be able to find a job that you don't mind so much—or maybe one you even really enjoy.

> **Definition**
> An allowance is an amount of money that someone (usually a parent) provides on a regular basis as spending money.

Getting a job as a teenager can have many benefits. Yes, of course, you're earning money—which is always nice, but you also learn how to budget, save, and manage your money. Learning those money lessons will help you figure out ways to stretch that paycheck as far as you can. When you get a job, you will become more "financially savvy," learning about life's little surprises, such as taxes, withholdings, and social security. Your first job (and your first paycheck) is basically a crash course in Accounting 101. But you want to make sure you don't crash and burn by making money and then spending it all with nothing to show for it. That's why you're reading this book!

Of course, having a job can have benefits other than money. You learn how to be responsible and dependable and all of those traits that will be very important to you as an adult. Also, you will probably develop some skills that will help you both in school and a career—such as how to communicate with people, manage your time, and stay calm in stressful situations.

GIGS AND OCCASIONAL WORK VS. OFFICIAL JOBS

The work options available to you will usually fall into one of two types. There's the type that often consists of "gigs" or occasional work—jobs such as babysitting, mowing lawns, and even an actual "gig" (the 1920s abbreviation for musical engagement) if you happen to play in a band.

Then there is the more formal type of job, such as being a cashier at a store or restaurant. Here you have a regular schedule and usually work a certain number of hours per week.

There are important differences between the two. With the occasional/gig type of work, you are often paid cash and aren't on an official payroll (this is why this type of work is often referred to as "off the books"). You usually don't have any deductions (money) taken out for taxes or other expenses. From a budget standpoint, a bad thing is that you often don't know when (or if) you will work, so there's no way to predict how much money you will earn, which can make it hard to figure out how you will pay your expenses or buy the things you want.

With a formal ("real") job, on the other hand, you are an official employee on the payroll. You will probably have taxes and possibly other deductions such as payment for health benefits or retirement accounts taken out of your paycheck. While this can be a bummer, it gets you familiar with the way your paycheck will look as an adult. In addition to taxes, you'll have to face other official duties of a formal job, such as going through an interview process, job application, tax paperwork, and other boring details.

> *"If your expenses are greater than your money, you have two choices: cut expenses or get a job."*.
> » Kristl Story, TheBudgetDiet.com

On the plus side, as an official employee, you are entitled to more protections and other safeguards thanks to Uncle Sam and all of his rules that tell companies how they can and cannot treat employees. Also, formal jobs are more likely to look good on your resume down the line.

If you're on the payroll with a formal job, in most cases, you must earn at least minimum wage. (There are exceptions, such as if you work as a waiter/waitress or another job where you receive tips.) The current federal minimum wage is $7.25 per hour, but some states have their own minimum wage, which is higher—and that trumps the federal minimum wage. For example, in Oregon, the minimum wage is $8.50 an hour.

HOW TO FIND A JOB

Okay, so you already know you want a job. Now how do you find one? That can sometimes be the hard part, especially if you live in an area where there aren't a lot of stores or businesses. You may need to do some legwork and spend time asking around and spreading the word, telling everyone you know that you're looking for leads on part-time jobs.

CLASSIFIED ADS

Traditionally, this was where your parents always went to look for a job. But times have changed, and the "Help Wanted" sections of most papers are pretty skimpy these days— and in fact, newspapers in general have gotten pretty thin. It's still worth skimming them, especially in the local town newspapers, because occasionally, you will find an ad seeking a babysitter or help with lawn work. When in doubt, you can always try Craiglist.org, the free online classified Web site, which basically killed the newspaper industry by taking away all of its profits from job advertisements. This is one of those good news/bad news things, however. The good news is that there are lots of local postings on Craiglist and other online classified advertising Web sites, especially if you live in a major area with its own section on the site. The bad news is that these sites are notoriously packed with scams and shady characters. You really need to use extreme caution when considering replying to any of these ads. Be very careful about revealing your personal information—and never agree to meet someone alone. (This might be one area to get your parents involved.)

EXPERT ADVICE!
Do get a job as soon as you turn 16. You don't need to commit to a 40-hour work week of manual labor, but why not spend a few hours a week doing something you enjoy doing—and get paid for it? Love reading? Apply at the local bookstore or library. Can't get by without your daily dose of caffeine? Be a barista and start slinging drinks! The best part: Most jobs offer a discount so you'll save on what you're already buying.
~ Jackie Warrick, President & Chief Savings Officer at CouponCabin.com

BULLETIN BOARDS

Like classified ads, bulletin boards may not be as common or helpful as they once were, but they are still worth checking out. Your odds of success can improve greatly, depending on the location of the bulletin board. If you live in a private development or gated community, for example, there may be a clubhouse or community center where people will often post notices seeking babysitters. Likewise, if your school has a bulletin board, you may spot notices of people seeking tutors.

TEEN-ORIENTED JOB SITES

With classified sections in newspapers nearly extinct, adults now find many of their jobs through online career sites like Monster.com, career sections of company Web sites, and social networking. For teens, these are worth checking out, but depending on the type of job you're seeking, you may be wasting your time. (You aren't likely to find many "official" job listings for babysitters, for example.) But never fear, recently a few Web sites have cropped up geared toward teen employment, including Teens4Hire.org (www.teens4hire. org) and Cool Works.com, which specializes in jobs in the outdoors, such as summer camps and at National Parks.. Other teen-oriented job sites include Snagajob.com—which specializes in jobs where you're paid by the hour and summer jobs. For a more formal job seeker, you might try www.studentjobs.gov—a Web site that features internships and jobs for students within the federal government.

TWITTER™ AND FACEBOOK

You use social networks like Twitter and Facebook for just about everything else, so why not take advantage of this resource to help find a job? Let your friends know you're looking for work or ask if they know anyone who is hiring. (Be sure to return the favor and pass along any leads that may be of interest to your friends.)

WORD OF MOUTH

Don't overlook the network of offline contacts you may have available—family and friends, people your parents may know, people from church or any clubs you belong to, and teachers/professors. All of these people are potential sources of jobs—and they will likely be impressed by your ambition to try to find a job.

COMMON JOBS FOR TEENS

BABYSITTING

Babysitting is one of the most common ways for teens to earn extra money. The good news is that it's fairly easy to find this type of job. Pretty much every parent with little kids needs a babysitter at some point. If you mention to everyone you know that you're available to babysit, you'll probably quickly find yourself with potential jobs.

There are some things you need to consider before seeking a babysitting job, though. First, obviously, you really need to like kids. You must have patience and be able to stay cool under stress. And you'll need a lot of energy! If you are creative and can come up with fun activities to do with kids, that will be a big help.

You also want to be very careful about choosing the people with whom you'll work. You don't want to just go into a stranger's home. The best bet is to stick with people your parents or other relatives already know. Otherwise, make sure your parents meet them first.

You also want to make sure you are prepared to handle an emergency. Make sure you become familiar with the home, so you'll know how to get the kids out quickly in case of fire or other emergency. Get the parents' cell phone numbers and a list of emergency contacts. Be sure to find out if the kids have allergies, medical conditions, or anything else you need to know. It's also a very good idea to take a first aid and CPR course, or even a "babysitting certification" course. Many hospitals offer these, or you can check with your local Red Cross.

Do's and Dont's of Being a Good Babysitter

Do plan to arrive early. This gives you enough time to set your stuff down and get the rundown from parents before they leave at their appointed hour. A little bit of initiative goes a long way in the babysitting world.

Do bring your own supplies, like books, paper, crayons, string, cards, and scissors, so that you don't have to ask the parents for anything. This way, you are armed with a few hours' worth of entertainment that can help you get off to a good start. If you give the kids some of your own supplies, it makes them feel that much more special.

Do look out for the kids' safety.

Do keep in contact with the parents. You'll have a half-dozen ways to communicate with them anyway, between Facebook, Twitter, and e-mail.

Do enjoy some family-friendly activities.

Do your best to be patient with the kids. You'll finally get the younger siblings you never had! Unless you already do have some, of course!

Do pay attention to the use of technology in the home. Do the kids have cell phones? Are they on the computer? If none of these apply, then DO NOT spend the whole time texting your friends because then the kids will only remember the fancy, enticingly digital things you did (texting, and so on) that they are not accustomed to seeing. (And besides, you shouldn't be distracted from paying attention to the kids.) By the same token, if the kids are allowed to be gadgetronic, give them that leeway but also try to encourage some old-school, wholesome, hands-on fun.

Don't allow the kids to watch anything violent, graphic, or otherwise disturbing. And you shouldn't be watching anything along those lines either while you're in the house, because the kids may be watching from the background. In other words, no Friday the 13th marathons.

Don't invite your friends or boyfriend or girlfriend to hang out with you for the night. Remember, you are working, not hanging out.

Don't throw a raging party that will make spacemen file a noise complaint because they can hear it from Neptune.

Don't use drugs or alcohol while on duty. (This should go without saying, but we'll say it anyway.)

Do have a set rate that you charge, so that you can quote if the parents ask. The rate will probably depend on the typical going rate in your area. If the parents simply pay you at the end of the night, take that amount and gauge whether the experience was worthwhile (monetarily and otherwise). It doesn't happen all the time, but some babysitters can be taken advantage of if they're not confident and savvy at the outset.

Do be gracious and respectful of people's homes and things.

Do feel free to do things like straighten up a room full of toys and do the dishes—don't go overboard though; because this can sometimes feel like an invasion of privacy for some people.

MOWING LAWNS

> **TIP**
>
> Gauge how your client likes his or her lawn done by taking a look at flower beds, state of the house, state of the car—if all of these things are highly manicured, then be sure to do an especially attentive job; it will be appreciated. (Although that doesn't mean you can slack off otherwise.) Also, if you do not do a job up to your clients' standards, then that is the only thing they will notice and remember about you.

Yard work may seem like a simple way to make money, but it can be harder than it seems. It's a good idea to practice on your own yard first to make sure you know exactly what's involved.

Mowing lawns and doing other types of yard work is physical labor. You will need lots of energy and must enjoy working outdoors (and can't mind getting dirty). On the plus side, you get to be outside on nice days, and you will probably get a good workout. When looking for potential customers, try people in your neighborhood. Good candidates are those who work a lot and don't have much time to spend on their yards. Also, the elderly often need help with these types of chores because they may be physically unable to do it on their own.

You will need to decide whether you will be using your own machine or not and what that means in terms of your clients' locations. If you are using your own machine, bear in mind that you'll have to carry or move it yourself and buy your own gas. If this is the case, be sure to factor that into your bill. If you're going to use your client's machine (which has its pros and cons—you may not be familiar with the machine, but at least you won't have to schlep it), then you should probably charge a lower rate.

RUNNING ERRANDS

Some people need help running errands, such as the elderly or those who have medical problems that make it difficult for them to leave the house. However, clients may also be busy people who work a lot or mothers with small children at home who don't want the hassle of finding a babysitter or dragging the kids out of the house.

One big consideration involved with running errands is transportation. If you don't have a car and a client wants you to pick up a bunch of groceries, you may have a problem. If you have a vehicle and will be using it to do these errands, make sure to factor the cost of gas and any other expenses into your fee.

Regardless of the mode of transportation, be efficient but not to the point of craziness: there's no reason to run from place to place and risk breaking things and being sloppy. Be aware that you're on the clock, but you also need to be careful.

If running errands becomes a by-product of lawn and housework gigs, then be sure to charge by the hour, rather than per job. This says to the client that you are flexible in terms of responsibilities, but you have your act together and want to get paid a fair rate for the work you do.

PET-SITTING: WHO LET THE DOGS OUT?

This can be a great part-time job, but it may not pay a ton of money. But it is a fantastic opportunity to prove how responsible you are—and DO NOT take a pet-sitting job if you are not responsible because there are lives at stake, LITERALLY. If you do show that you are capable and can become friends with the animals in question, then you can quickly become priceless to the pet owners. Knowing that there is someone trustworthy and available makes going away that much easier for pet owners.

> **TIP**
>
> See if there's anything else the clients might want you to do while they're gone—does the mail need to be collected, trash taken out, garden watered? All of these extras will make you the model sitter and the first person they'll call whenever they might need help.

People are very specific about their pets, so if some sort of instruction sheet is left, adhere to it. If the pet owners do not provide written instructions, it's probably a good idea to bring a pen and notebook along the first time you meet with them to make sure you retain all the relevant information (and also to demonstrate that you're taking the job seriously). Before your first official day on the job, see if you can set up a brief meeting time at their house, so that your clients can walk you through where everything is and show you what they need you to do for their pet(s). This is also a good opportunity to talk about payment. You will want to consider how much time and work is involved when considering a rate. Dogs need to be walked several times a day, which can take time and energy. So you may want to charge by the day or based on how many times you need to walk the dog. Fish are easy and don't take too much time, so maybe a lump sum for the entire length of time the owner is gone is a better way to handle a job like that.

RESTAURANT JOBS: THE BEST KIND OF TIPS

Restaurants can offer a variety of jobs that can often be good choices for teens. Restaurants love a worker with experience, but also someone who is ready and willing to learn new things.

Being a server—more often than not—generates the most amount of income because you have a set hourly rate plus whatever tips are earned. Different restaurants handle tips differently, so it's good to know the possible scenarios beforehand. Some allow servers to keep everything they earn and take it home at the end of the night, but in this situation the server often earns a lower wage rate because it's expected that he or she will supplement the missing wages with tips. Other restaurants "pool" tips, which means that all of the tips that everyone earns get combined into a lump amount that then gets disbursed evenly among everyone in the restaurant. (In other words, all tips combine to make one big pizza and everyone gets a slice.) This situation is better for people who are not servers, and it often creates a sense of camaraderie among the staff because there is a level playing field. But it can also cause resentment among servers who may not be eager to share their tips.

Dishwashing is a job that is necessary at every restaurant and a great way to show that you aren't lazy. Though it's not the most glamorous of jobs, it's probably the least demanding in terms of time commitment and therefore ideal for someone trying to earn money while in school or working another job. However, it can be physically demanding, and you may need to work at a very fast pace.

Hosting (being the front-of-house person who shows customers to their seats, makes a waiting list, etc.) is another good way to be earning extra money without the time and effort that being a server often requires. A friendly attitude, organization skills, and time management are all necessary components of being an effective host.

Unless you are a server or a bartender, restaurant jobs can be a great way to supplement other jobs or school-life because the time commitment is generally not too demanding and it is a great way to get some experience and extra money.

As with any job, responsibility for your role is key and must be treated with an air of professionalism. Do not forget to call before you're going to be late or not make a shift; do everything you can to find someone to cover your shift; and be upfront about when you'll be able to work and the time when you know you won't be able to work. Dress appropriately. Do not alienate yourself from your fellow staff—they are your peers and your (potential) friends.

EXPERT ADVICE!

"Having a car is a major expense for most teens. My parents taught me a great lesson when I was looking to buy my first car. I began working when I was 14 years old. My family owned an appliance business, and I delivered and set up appliances during my summer break. My parents agreed to match the amount I earned, and I could apply this towards my car. Instead of hanging out with my friends all summer, I lifted heavy appliances in the hot Florida sun. I continued to do this in the afternoons once school started. By the time I turned 16, I had saved $2,000! With my parents matching this amount, I had enough to buy a $4,000 car. My grandfather was looking to purchase a new vehicle and was kind enough to sell me his truck for the amount I had. This was my first real understanding of money. I realized that if I worked hard and saved, I could buy something that I desired. I was fortunate that my parents gave me money, but even more fortunate that they made me work to earn this amount. Some of my friends had their cars and other items bought for them by their parents and, let me tell you, they did not treat their possessions like I did mine. I valued what I had because I knew how much sweat had gone into earning it."

~ Danny Kofke, special education teacher and author of "A Simple Book of Financial Wisdom: Teach Yourself (and Your Kids) How to Live Wealthy with Little Money" (Wyatt-MacKenzie, September 2011)

RETAIL JOBS: TIME FOR THE BIG SALE

Working at a store is a popular job choice for many teens. For one thing, many young people spend a lot of their time at the mall or other stores anyway, so they figure they may as well get paid for it. However, that attitude can often backfire on you. There's a big difference between hanging out at The Gap and working there. In fact, employers are often afraid of hiring teens who seem eager to just hang out and chat with friends on company time.

Retail jobs can offer a chance for promotion. In many instances, workers who are lower on the totem pole can transition to become managers and supervisors, meaning more responsibility and trust and (often) more money. You can often climb the company ladder fairly quickly, depending on how flexible and hard-working you are. You will earn points by showing your willingness to do whatever you are assigned to, whether it's folding sweaters, shelving books, bagging groceries, or vacuuming the store. It's important to take pride in your work and be efficient while remaining thorough and friendly.

Many retail jobs require workers to observe some sort of dress code, and you shouldn't ignore this. In many cases, you can use a little creativity to be stylish and unique while still adhering to the dress code.

Big stores often require an official application and some sort of interview process as well as references. Teachers, neighbors, pastors, coaches, and band leaders are all good sources for recommendations. Do not be scared off by the application; if there is a high degree of professionalism and an official nature to the process, it often means that there is a set wage in place and less of a chance of being taken advantage of. Also, big stores often have bonuses and scholarship programs for kids in high school, which is basically like being recognized for earning money for college, and then being given more money to put towards college. This can be a great perk.

As with any job, take a retail job seriously and be enthusiastic and willing to accomplish (conquer!) any task set forth before you.

WORKIN' AT THE CAR WASH, YEAH!

Working at a car wash offers many of the same pros and cons as yard work—especially if you are working for an outdoor car wash. It's definitely hard work, but you will get to be outdoors in nice weather. Outdoor car washes are seasonal businesses, though, since they are often closed during the coldest months. So this may not be a good source of year-round work.

THINGS TO CONSIDER WITH A PART-TIME JOB

> **TIP**
>
> Don't limit yourself to one part-time job or type of job. You may need to piece together a few gigs in order to get a decent amount of cash in your pocket each week. For example, maybe you can babysit one or two nights a week, mow a few lawns on weekends, and run some errands occasionally in between.

If you are in high school, visit your guidance office to inquire about working papers and whether you will need them (the laws vary from state to state). There are also many laws in place that limit the number of hours and conditions in which teenagers can work, so be sure to know about what your employers can and cannot ask, and whether you will even be allowed to do the jobs you are *considering*. For example, construction and other hard labor jobs, jobs with large machines and blades, and any jobs that involve being around alcohol are often off-limits for teens. For more information about teens and working, check out the Occupational Safety and Health Administration's Rules for Teen and Youth Worker Rules Sheet: http://www.ehso.com/oshateen.php.

Going to school and holding a job at the same time can be a great way to learn effective time management, but bear in mind that school needs to take priority. You need to do well in school in order to either continue your education at college or get a good start on a career.

"I started working when I was 15, doing pickup babysitting jobs, lawn jobs, and then waitressing at the local diner on the weekends. This meant that I always had my own money and was not beholden to anyone. But as the pressure from school and extracurricular activities increased, I found myself stretched a little too thin. I asked my mom for advice, and she told me something that I think still rings true for anyone of that age. She said, "School is your job." Though it sounded glib and tacky at the time, it has rung true time and again throughout college and in the few years beyond. If I had let school suffer for the sake of earning a few dollars, I would not have done well in school, and would not have learned the skills that inform the degree that I use every day in the job that I got because of my educational background. I held work-study jobs all through college, which gave me discretionary funds, but also forced me to focus because I had to manage my time most efficiently in order to make room for both school and work. But if I had not treated school as seriously as I treated my jobs, I would not have been able to get the good job—with benefits—that I have today."

~ *Railey Savage, age 20-something*

GETTING PAID (AND BEING PREPARED FOR YOUR FIRST PAYCHECK)

Getting your very first paycheck can be an exciting moment—and it can also be a big shock, as the amount you actually get may be less than what you expected.

When getting the stub from your first paycheck, do not be alarmed by how much money seems to be missing. While it may seem totally unfair, withholding (money being deducted from paychecks for things like Social Security and Medicare and taxes) is a required part of work. Depending on your situation and how much money you earn, you or your parents may get some or all of the taxes that were withheld back in the form of a refund from the government when you file a tax return at the end of the year.

If at all possible, it is best to have your paychecks directly deposited in the bank, eliminating the possibility of losing a check, forgetting to deposit it, or giving in to temptation and simply cashing it, rather than depositing it and building up your savings. Many banks also offer special perks if you use direct deposit because it's a sign that you are a guaranteed customer who will be using that account a lot.

Your paycheck is your opportunity to see that your work and time were worth something. Be conscious of how many hours you have worked and whether you called in sick or worked overtime—all of these are factors that affect how much you earn per pay period. You should not be surprised by the amount of your checks.

Be aware that many employers do not like employees to work overtime (there may be laws against teenagers working much more than a certain amount of time, anyway) because they don't like paying the overtime rates usually required by law. That being said, be sure you are paid for EVERY INSTANCE that you work. You should never be working for free—if you did the work, you deserve to be paid for it.

ONE WAY TO BEAT THE SUMMER JOB BLUES— WORK FROM HOME

With about 1.1 million teens applying for jobs each summer, the competition for the typical teen job at fast food restaurants or retail shops is fierce. So to make sure you beat the summer job blues, you might try to harness the power of technology to try alternative ways of working, such as telecommuting.

For years, adults have been working full-time jobs from the comfort of their own home. This is called telecommuting or working virtually. As a teen, you probably wouldn't want a full-time telecommuting job since you're still in school. But there are lots of ways you can earn extra spending money by working from home on a part-time basis. All you need is a computer, a reliable Internet connection or phone, and some time, and you've got a winning formula. From designing and creating Web sites to answering simple phone surveys, technology has provided myriad ways for teens to earn money without ever leaving their home. The following are some work opportunities that allow you work from home. But beware, there are plenty of work-at-home scams that earn you very little money and may even ask you to spend money. Stay away from those!

Pros and Cons of Working from Home

Pros:

You set your own schedule. The more you work, the more you earn.

No transportation issues or expenses.

No worries about wardrobe or dress code.

Cons:

You don't get acclimated to a typical work environment.

You don't learn interpersonal/office sills.

May not have an opportunity to earn references for future employment.

It can be lonely!

WORK-AT-HOME OPPORTUNITY: FOCUS GROUPS

When a company is ready to launch a new product or make other types of business decisions, its marketing department sometimes decides to test the waters by gathering up a group of people who represent the company's consumers. This is called a focus group or a test panel. With more than $91 billion in income earned annually, teens are especially in demand with lots of companies who focus on consumer products such as clothing and electronics. These companies are dying to know what appeals to students like you—and how to get you to buy their stuff.

"I have made quite a bit of cash doing focus groups. I went to one where all I had to do was talk about chewing gum to an anthropologist for 2 hours, and I made $200 in cash. I also got to watch a World Cup Game on a 3D TV for $25. While the big-paying surveys only come around every few months, it's nice to have a little extra cash for just sharing my thoughts. "
~ *Lindsay Long, Austin, Texas*

WORK-AT-HOME OPPORTUNITY: ONLINE SURVEYS

You've got lots of opinions, and you love sharing them. That makes you a perfect candidate to do online surveys. There are often opportunities for teens to take surveys related to electronics, online games, entertainment, and other youth-focused topics. Some survey sites will pay you in gift cards instead of cash, so make sure you know how you will be rewarded for your opinions.

Here are Web addresses of some cash-paying survey sites:

http://www.pineconeresearch.com/

https://www.mysurvey.com

https://www.opinionoutpost.com/

You can also look for product-testing offers, because then you get things like shampoo, paper towels, and pasta sauce for free—all things that you would normally spend money on.

A note of precaution: You should check with your parents first before you provide any contact information on any of these sites.

WORK-AT-HOME OPPORTUNITY: ONLINE WRITING

Love English class? Want to make a little cash showing off your AP English skills? Then try writing online. The Internet has created an explosion in content demand. With Google's and Yahoo!'s computerized spiders seeking good content, companies are clamoring to fill their Web pages with articles, and they're willing to pay anyone who can deliver. Age doesn't matter, only delivery does. The money isn't grand—sometimes it's as low as $1 an article—but if you get proficient at it, you can whip out the necessary wordsmithing without breaking a sweat yet earning a few dollars for your little effort. Some Web sites that are always looking for writers include:

Yahoo! Voices, formerly Associated Content:
http://voices.yahoo.com/

Helium:
http://www.helium.com/

Triond:
https://www.triond.com/

WORK-AT-HOME OPPORTUNITY: FREELANCE PROGRAMMING

The Internet, with its endless potential and new opportunities, has eliminated countless barriers to earning money. Thanks to the democratization of the economy, factors such as race, income, and even age are no longer obstacles to earning cash. And one place this economic equalization is realized is in the computer programming sector. In the past, you needed a master's degree from an institution like Stanford to be even considered in the computer technology world. But the spread of the Internet has made computer technology mainstream, and now even those with rudimentary tech skills can earn a living building Web sites, running help desks, and repairing computers. If you have a knack for programming and design or know HTML, Ruby on Rails, or any other Web-focused programming language, you can make a bundle working from a laptop and your bedroom. Check out these Web sites for potential jobs:

Scriptlance, recently acquired by Freelancer.com, is geared toward the entrepreneurial programmer: www.freelancer.com

Odesk.com, one of the largest virtual freelance communities out there, also looks for programmers: www.odesk.com

Getacoder.com—need we say more? http://www.getacoder.com/

OTHER "AT-HOME" OPPORTUNITIES

There are some of us who would love to work at home on a regular basis but just do not have the time, and that's just fine. There are other "at home" opportunities where you can earn money without all that sweating of the brow effort.

THE GARAGE SALE

This is an oldie but goodie. It's the classic way to make some extra bucks quickly. Most likely, you've got lots of stuff in your closet or attic you don't use anymore. You can make this a family project—your parents will probably be happy to clear out some junk from the house as well. You may even want to get some of your friends involved—the more cool stuff you have, the better.

The key to a successful yard sale is promotion. Even if you have the greatest stuff in the world, you won't make any money if nobody shows up. You have to do everything you can to attract customers. Put an ad in the newspaper. Hang signs with colorful balloons throughout the neighborhood. Promote your sale via social networks. Be sure to mention any unusual or unique items that may catch people's attention. Join a community yard sale sponsored by your neighborhood—you'll probably have more traffic.

SELL STUFF ON eBay

eBay is the online version of a yard sale. The advantages are that you don't have strangers wandering around your yard—and your potential customers are lots of people all over the world. The downside: There is more work involved, and it may take some time for you to conduct the auction and then wait for the payment to arrive. Still, you can make more profit through eBay because you have a bigger audience. You aren't limited to the bargain hunters who tend to cruise garage sales locally.

TIP
You can view similar items that have sold recently on eBay to get an estimate of what your stuff may sell for.

You must be prepared to invest some time in your eBay endeavor. You have to take pictures of your items and then write up descriptions that make the item sound as tempting as possible. You also need to communicate with potential buyers and maybe answer questions about your item. When the auction is over, you need to package the item up and ship it off to the buyer. So it takes some time and effort to build an eBay empire, but you can pocket some pretty nice profits, especially if you have in-demand items like collectibles, designer clothes, or electronics.

"One thing that I have done in the past is going shopping at a place like Marshalls or TJMaxx, and when I find a designer item for very cheap, I buy and then resell it on eBay. Or if I know there is a hot item such as the Wii Fit, I'll buy two and sell one on eBay. If I'm lucky, it'll cover the cost of both items, and it's like I got mine for free!"

~ Lindsay Long, Austin, Texas

SELL CRAFTS AND OTHER ITEMS ONLINE

Have a knack for making crafts? You may be able to make money by selling your creations online. Etsy (www.etsy.com) is one of the biggest online sites to sell crafts and other homemade items. You can set up your own store with pictures of your items. If you're under 18, you can sell stuff on Etsy as long as you have a parent's permission. The site does take a small cut of the money you get, but on the plus side, you have privacy protection because buyers never have your personal contact information.

WePay (www.wepay.com) is a site that allows you to set up an online store page or site easily (no HTML or code skills required) and collect payments. The site takes a small cut of the money you make.

SELL YOUR PHOTOS

If you have some photo equipment (or at least a pretty good camera) and an eye for getting some cool shots, you can sell your photos online. Right now, there is a high demand for good images because lots of people are starting blogs or Web sites and need photos to accompany the text. The amount you make for each photo can vary from around 25 cents to several dollars or more. The good news: You can sell each image as many times as you want, so this can be an ongoing source of income. Check out sites like Shutterstock or iStockPhoto to find out how to sell your photos.

YOUTUBE VIDEOS

These days, just about everyone knows how to make a video, even if it's just a basic one taken with a Flip video camera or your smartphone. But if you're an aspiring filmmaker, you don't need to graduate from an expensive film school to make some money with your videos. YouTube has a "partners program" that allows people to earn money by putting ads on their videos or on the pages near the videos. They look for users who have a lot of fans, so you have the best chance of a good payday with this method if you can get lots of people to watch your videos or if you can come up with funny or unique ideas that will get attention through word-of-mouth.

WEB DESIGN

As we've already mentioned, lots of people are starting Web sites these days to promote their business or just share information (or opinions) on whatever topic interests them. But for people who aren't totally comfortable with technology, the idea of making a Web site can be intimidating. They will often gladly pay someone else to do it, especially someone who can do it quickly and maybe add some cool design elements or features. If you happen to know HTML, you'll really have an advantage, but there are many design programs out there that allow you to create Web sites even without HTML.

START YOUR OWN WEB SITE OR BLOG

> **Note:**
> You may need to set up a PayPal account in order to get paid, as some online companies send payment via PayPal. This is quick and easy but you will have to have a bank account to set up a Paypal account.

Creating Web sites for other people is one way to make money. But another option is to just create a Web site of your own. If you have a cool concept or can gather up a following that brings your site a lot of traffic, you can then sell ads on your site. You can offer businesses the opportunity to place an ad on your site. (Obviously, you'll want to make sure it's a legit business and the ad doesn't contain anything objectionable.) If you can show stats that prove how many visitors your site gets, it will be easier to get advertisers. Google has a program called Google Ads, which is an easy way for you to put ads on your site and get paid for it. (The amount you earn depends on the number of people who visit your site and click on the ad. Most people don't make a ton of money, but it doesn't require a lot of work on your part.)

GAMING FOR REAL BUCKS

If you like playing video games, you may have found yourself wishing you could find a way to do it for a living. Well, there may soon be a way for you to make some cash as a gamer. Blizzard Entertainment recently launched an online video game called Diablo 3. One unique aspect of this game is that it offers an auction marketplace where people can earn virtual items that they can then sell for real money. Check the rules and regulations, as the real-money auction does have restrictions.

TUTORING

If you get good grades or tend to be really smart in a certain subject, you can make some money by helping other students (or sometimes even adults) master topics in that subject. Most of the large, major tutoring services require tutors to have a college degree, so your best bet is probably to think small and local: Spread the word that you are seeking tutoring clients or post a notice on your social networks. To avoid having strangers come to your house, plan ways that allow you to do the tutoring at a local library or quiet meeting spot or even by phone or online. If you have Skype, that may also be an option.

SHARE AND SHARE ALIKE: MAKING MONEY IN THE SHARING ECONOMY

In the poem, "All I Really Need to Know I Learned in Kindergarten," Robert Fulghum offers some sage advice for those looking to simplify their life. He posits such gems as "Don't hit people," "Play fair," and "Flush," as words to live by. But though this is all great advice, there are two words he says that may mean more to you than just a carefree life. The two words—Share Everything—could mean cold, hard cash, thanks to a changing economy.

In preschool, when you shared, you just had to give up your toy for a few minutes so that the boy with the runny nose could have some fun with it, too. But in an economy that's in recession, sharing can turn into quite a lucrative business. In fact, millions of Americans are taking the items they already own and sharing them for a fee.

You've heard of eBay, where sellers from all over the world sell their goods to people who may want and need them. Well, many buyers got disenchanted with eBay—they no longer wanted to buy; they only wanted to rent.

After the 2008 financial crisis, a new crop of online merchants arrived on the scene. These people weren't exactly selling their stuff so much as loaning it. From Prada handbags, to Gucci shoes, the rent economy gave birth to a new way of shopping that allows neighbors to fulfill requests that were previously only resolved by going to the mall.

This type of "loaning" or "sharing" for a fee gained a boost with the robust use of social networking. Now people aren't just wasting time reading the Newsfeed on Facebook; they're actually finding ways to rent out that dusty guitar that has been sitting in the basement for $50 a day or even loaning their dog to lonely would-be pet owners for a nice fee of $25.

In what's called the "sharing economy," people are literally sharing everything they own—from their car, to their bikes, to their skills and talents, all for a reasonable fee. And if you're creative enough, you could make as much as $1,000 a month simply by sharing what already belongs to you.

Also called "collaborative consumption," this new way of buying and selling has turned the old free market on its head. In the sharing economy, it doesn't matter what your credit score is; it only matters how many good reviews you've gotten as a seller or buyer. The use of social networks in the companies that cater to this type of money-making venture is extremely important in building a good online reputation.

The sharing economy is also a virtual one, as it operates almost entirely in the online space. From Freecycle.com, to Air BnB, where strangers pay other strangers to stay in their homes just like a hotel, you have to be online to get in on this economy.

SO HOW DOES THIS ALL WORK?

Put simply, a user (we'll call her Abby) wants something she doesn't currently have to use on a temporary basis. Abby would go online to a collaborative consumption company such as Air BnB, or taskrabbit.com, or Zaarly.com. She would then post what she needs and what she's willing to pay. The owner decides whether to accept the deal. Negotiations are made, the company gets a small transaction fee, and the user and the owner both go away happy.

So how can teens take advantage of this sharing economy? Easily. Just think of the Internet as a big playground where the haves and the have-nots bargain over 1's and 0's to meet supply and demand.

Turn that occasional lawn mowing gig or babysitting work into a money-making empire with the assistance of online companies catering to the enterprising individual looking to provide labor.

> # TIP
> "Zaarly can be a time saver by providing assistance with tasks such as dog walking, dropping off and picking up dry cleaning, flower delivery, and picking up last-minute gifts."
> ~ *Self-described busy mom Leticia Barr and blogger at www.techsavvymamma.com*

For example. Zaarly is a Web site and mobile application that allows local people to sell and buy from each other. Many people use apps such as Zaarly to find teenagers just like you to do what teenagers do best—run errands! Why run errands for mom and dad for free when others will pay you for it? Love to walk dogs? Like getting groceries for senior citizens? Don't mind dropping off and picking up dry cleaning? Why not do it all for a small fee? At Web sites like Zaarly.com and taskrabbit.com, you can find willing buyers right in your neighborhood.

Remember to stick to the usual safety precautions—make sure your parents know whom you're dealing with, and do not meet a person without bringing a caring adult along for the first visit—and you've got a way to earn some extra dough.

Want a roster of babysitting clients that have been reviewed and evaluated by your peers? Then sign up at www.sittingaround.com, a babysitting co-op that offers teens a booking calendar, potential clients, access to a background check, and other administrative services to help you build a nice clientele.

Not into doing other's dirty work? Don't want to break a sweat? No problem—just raid your closet and gather all your old toys, and rent them by the month at www.rentthattoy. com! Forget your little brother; turn your hand-me-downs into cash.

From college textbooks, to old toys, and even to your dog Fluffy, in the sharing economy, you can make money with just about anything, and you're only limited by your imagination. Still, here is a list of possible share items anyway and a list of places where you can make money by loaning, renting out, or sharing your skills, possessions, or even talent. Share and share alike, and who knows—you may become rich. (As with any online company, please read the terms of the service agreement and get your parent's permission if you're under age 18).

BEST ITEMS/SKILL TO SHARE/SELL AND MAKE MONEY

Toys	Car
Clothes	Books
Musical instruments	CD's, tapes, records, videos, DVD's, Blu-Ray
Anything by Apple	Lego sorting (actual request from taskrabitt. com you could earn up to $50!)

Doing laundry

Washing dishes

Returning baby gifts

Picking up groceries

Writing letters

Survey just about anything-daycare centers, stores, etc.,

Advise out-of-towners on child-friendly activities in your hometown (actual request from taskrabitt.com!)

Bikes

Helmets

Skateboards

Purses, handbags,

That extra space in your parent's house (well, maybe not, but you can always ask!!!)

ONLINE SHARING/RENTING SITES

www.snapgoods.com

www.zaarly.com

www.taskrabitt.com

www.rentthattoy.com

www.sittingaround.com

www.spinlister.com (bikes)

www.airbnb.com

For more information on how to navigate the share economy, read the online mag: http://www.shareable.net/

QUIZ: WHAT TYPE OF HOME-BASED JOB WOULD BE YOUR BEST FIT?

Things That Describe You	Job
Outgoing, Wise, Condescending, Whimsical, Can Operate a Keyboard Better Than a Circus Chimp	Blogger
Thrifty, Hoarder, Collector, Detached, Have Access to Your Sister's CD Collection	eBay Seller
Energetic, Friendly, Outdoorsy, Charitable, Able to Appear Busier Than You Actually Are	Odd Jobs Around Town
Charismatic, Chatty, Unique, Popular, Funny, Ready to Sing in Front of a Camera	YouTube partner
Helpful, Warm, Patient, Clever, Knowledgeable, Desire to Feel Smarter Than Anybody Else	Tutor
Dedicated, Flexible, Thoughtful, Opinionated, Like to Click Boxes and Answer Questions	Survey Taker

WATCH OUT FOR WORK-AT-HOME SCAMS!

There are lots of legitimate ways to earn money from home. Unfortunately, there are also lots of scams and crooks who just want to rip you off or get your money. Watch out for places that want to charge you money for "leads" or sell you a directory of companies that use home workers. Never give out your credit card number (or your parents' credit card number).

CROSSWORD: WORKING WORLD

ACROSS

1. A Web site where you sell junk to the highest bidder.
4. The thing that lets you type great ideas on a blog.
8. The thing that earns you money; employment.
9. Having a lot of money; What Bill Gates is.
13. The source of all happiness; It makes the world go round.
14. The World Wide Web; It has everything.
16. They pop up on Web sites; Everyone hates them.
17. The money you get weekly for doing a good job.
18. What you are when you do a bad job; Donald Trump did it to everybody.
19. You never want to work during this; Christmas is one.
20. A place to keep money; The cheater is in charge of this in Monopoly.

DOWN

2. The one who yells at you all day during work.
3. A video Web site that has keyboard cats.
5. An online journal that anybody can write.
6. What you want to do when you're old and have enough money; Brett Favre did it four times.
7. You click it to use a computer; it hates cats.
10. The last day of the workweek. TGI this day!
11. The most famous search engine; You will use it to look up the other answers to this puzzle.
12. 100 dollar bills; Rappers think it is all about them.
15. What you take when you have time off from work.

CHAPTER 3
ANALYZING YOUR PAYCHECK

So you've joined the working world and are excited have begun to earn your own money. You count the days until payday and eagerly rip open the envelope with your paycheck (or check your bank balance online)—only to discover with great disappointment that the amount is much less than you had expected.

Before you call your employer to say there must have been some sort of mistake, you should take a good look at your paystub. This is the paper that is attached to your paycheck (or, if you get direct deposit, the paper that explains the amount of your deposit).

Be prepared: There may be some abbreviations and terms you've never heard of. For example, you may be thinking, "Who the heck is FICA, and why are they getting a chunk of my check?"

It's time for a little reality check: The sad, but true, fact is, when you earn money, you rarely actually get the entire amount you earn. There are some exceptions, such as freelance gigs or odd jobs, for which you are paid cash or "under the table" (and even then the IRS will demand its cut). But most of the time, there will be deductions taken out of your paycheck.

These deductions can be for a variety of things, including taxes, health insurance, and even charity donations.

WORKING FOR THE MAN: MANDATORY DEDUCTIONS

> The amount you earn *before* deductions (your hourly rate times the number of hours you work) is called your gross pay. The amount you actually receive *after* deductions is called your net pay.

There are some deductions that your employer is required to take out of your check. Neither you nor your employer has any choice about this—there is no getting around it.

Mandatory deductions are mainly in the form of taxes. Most likely, you will see several lines of tax deductions on your pay stub. These may include federal, state, and local taxes. (Sometimes, federal and state taxes aren't deducted if you make less than a certain amount per year.)

Employees also pay into the Social Security and Medicare programs. These may appear on your pay stub as FICA—which stands for Federal Insurance Contributions Act.

VOLUNTARY DEDUCTIONS

There are also voluntary deductions, ones that you choose to make. These would include items such as health coverage (if your employer offers it) and charity donations.

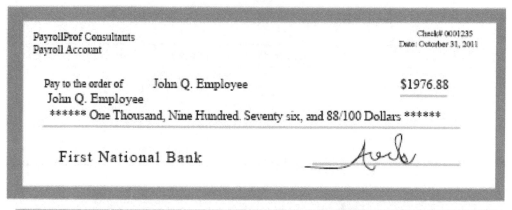

John Q. Employee			October 31, 2011
Gross Pay			$3000.00
Deductions			
	Federal Income Tax	$277.71	
	State Income Tax	$105.15	
	Social Security	$122.85	
	Medicare	$42.41	
	Insurance–Post Tax	$175.00	
	401k Plan	$200.00	
	Charity	$25.00	
	Flex Spending	$75.00	
	Total Deductions		$1023.12
	Net Pay		$1976.88

Source: Roger A. Smith, CPP
www.payrollprof.com

YEAR-TO-DATE TOTALS

Your pay stub will usually include a section with your year-to-date (YTD) totals. This makes it easy to see at a quick glance how much you have earned and paid in taxes so far this year.

Here's another sample of a pay stub, showing year-to-date totals.

123 - John R. Doe	Pay Period **11/7/11 to 11/18/11**			Required Deductions		
Earnings				Federal Income Tax	00.00	00.00
				FICA - Medicare	06.08	12.16
Hours 50	Rate 9.00	This Period 450.00	YTD 900.00	WI State Income Tax	00.00	00.00
				FICA - Social Security	25.92	51.84
Gross Pay		450.00	900.00	Other Deductions		
				Health Insurance	00.00	00.00
				401k	00.00	00.00
				Parking	00.00	00.00
				NET PAY	$418.00	$836.00

Your Employer
1234 Some Street
Milwaukee, WI ZIPCODE

Check Number: XXXXXX
Pay Date: **11/7/11**

PAY   ***Four hundred eighteen dollars and 00 cents************************$418.00

To the Order of
     John R. Doe
     555 Some Street
     Milwaukee, WI ZIP CODE

Source: TheMint.org

WHERE DOES THIS MONEY GO?

Congratulations, you are now a taxpayer! Most of the deductions from your paycheck are taxes that go to the government (either federal, state, or local) to fund various programs and services. These include everything from large national programs, like Homeland Security, to local services like pothole repairs.

Depending on how much you earn, you may be able to get some or all of your tax payments back in the form of a refund when you file your taxes at the end of the year. Your parents can help you with this.

When you first start working at a job, you will probably fill out a lot of paperwork. One form you'll no doubt complete is the IRS W-4 form. This is an important form and one that many people find confusing. The W-4 helps your employer figure out how much money to withhold from your paycheck for federal taxes.

On the W-4, you list the number of withholding allowances you want to claim. This is an IRS term that basically means how much money you want to go to the IRS towards your taxes. The more allowances you claim, the less money is withheld for taxes. If you claim zero allowances, your employer will hold the maximum amount from your check.

Why is this so important? If your employer doesn't withhold enough money from your paycheck to cover what you owe in taxes, you will end up owing the government money at the end of the year. On the other hand, if too much is withheld, you will get a tax refund. Most people think that's a good thing—but it really means that you've been giving the government an interest-free loan all year.

The IRS has a withholding allowance calculator on its Web site to help you determine what figure to enter on this line. "Using 2010 tax rates, a 16-year-old student can earn up to $11,100 with no federal income tax liability," says Bruce D. Kowal, Certified Public Accountant from www.KowalTaxClinic.com. "This is because of the Making Work Pay credit. However, this individual still has to pay social security taxes, which are automatically withheld—no choice here. So, if the student is earning less than $12,000, he or she can fill out the W-4 as single and zero allowances."

Here is what the W-4 form looks like:

-------------------------- Separate here and give Form W-4 to your employer. Keep the top part for your records. --------------------------

Form **W-4** Department of the Treasury Internal Revenue Service	**Employee's Withholding Allowance Certificate** ▶ Whether you are entitled to claim a certain number of allowances or exemption from withholding is subject to review by the IRS. Your employer may be required to send a copy of this form to the IRS.	OMB No. 1545-0074 20**12**

1 Your first name and middle initial	Last name	2 Your social security number
Home address (number and street or rural route)	3 ☐ Single ☐ Married ☐ Married, but withhold at higher Single rate. **Note.** If married, but legally separated, or spouse is a nonresident alien, check the "Single" box.	
City or town, state, and ZIP code	4 If your last name differs from that shown on your social security card, check here. You must call 1-800-772-1213 for a replacement card. ▶ ☐	

5	Total number of allowances you are claiming (from line **H** above **or** from the applicable worksheet on page 2)	**5**	
6	Additional amount, if any, you want withheld from each paycheck	**6**	$
7	I claim exemption from withholding for 2012, and I certify that I meet **both** of the following conditions for exemption.		
	• Last year I had a right to a refund of **all** federal income tax withheld because I had **no** tax liability, **and**		
	• This year I expect a refund of **all** federal income tax withheld because I expect to have **no** tax liability.		
	If you meet both conditions, write "Exempt" here . . . . ▶	**7**	

Under penalties of perjury, I declare that I have examined this certificate and, to the best of my knowledge and belief, it is true, correct, and complete.

Employee's signature
(This form is not valid unless you sign it.) ▶   Date ▶

8 Employer's name and address (Employer: Complete lines 8 and 10 only if sending to the IRS.)	9 Office code (optional)	10 Employer identification number (EIN)

For Privacy Act and Paperwork Reduction Act Notice, see page 2.   Cat. No. 10220Q   Form **W-4** (2012)

THE MOST COMMON PAYROLL DEDUCTIONS*

FEDERAL INCOME TAX

You can thank President Woodrow Wilson for all the money that gets taken out of your paycheck. Though the United States had levied taxes on its populous in wartime and peace time before the turn of the 20th century, it was the Sixteenth Amendment to the Constitution—passed in 1913 and championed by Wilson—that made the federal income tax permanent. This is a tax that employers are required to withhold from their employees' pay. Money collected is used to fund many national programs, such as defense, law enforcement, and general running of the country. The amount withheld is applied to an employee's annual tax liability itemized on the yearly tax return.

*[Source: Roger A. Smith, CPP; www.payrollprof.com]

STATE/LOCAL INCOME TAX

Similarly, states and many local taxing authorities also require employers to withhold income tax from their employees. These dollars are used to fund state and local programs, such as road maintenance, local law enforcement, and other state and local expenses. Before you moan about more taxes, remember that schools are also paid by taxes—property taxes. So the next time you pass a homeowner in your neighborhood, you might want to thank him or her for the new school cafeteria!

SOCIAL SECURITY TAX

Social Security Tax, also called FICA, is used to pay out federally provided retirement benefits to citizens who are at least 62 years old. It is also used to pay out benefits to disabled citizens who are unable to work. As of 2011, the rate for FICA taxes paid by employees was 4.2 percent of the first $106,000, plus 1.45 percent of the entire income. In past years, the employer would pay an equal amount to the employee's FICA payments. However, for the 2011 tax year, the employer paid an amount equivalent to 6.2 percent of the first $106,000 of the employee's salary toward social security compared to the 4.2 percent paid by the employee.

MEDICARE TAX

Medicare Tax is used to pay out federally provided health-care benefits for the citizens over age 65.

INSURANCE DEDUCTIONS

Currently, many employers offer employees the option to enroll themselves and their family members in a group health plan and/or group life insurance plans. These plans can be funded entirely by the employer (very rare), entirely by the employee, or by both the employer and employee. Depending on how the plan is constructed, employee dollars used to pay their portion of the health plan can be pre-tax contributions or post-tax contributions. Pre-tax contributions are dollars that are NOT added into the employee's taxable earnings used to calculate taxes. Here's a tip for teens: Before you sign up for health insurance with your employer, check with your parents to see if you're covered under their health insurance. If you are, keep a little more change in your pocket.

RETIREMENT SAVING PLAN DEDUCTIONS

It may sound crazy to think about retiring now, but if you want to be secure and happy after you've worked your last job, now is the time to start saving for that day. Many employers give employees the option to participate in various types of retirement savings plans. Like insurance plans, these plans can be funded entirely by the employer (e.g., pension plans), entirely by the employee, or by both the employer and employee. If your employer offers a retirement savings plan, pounce on it. The few dollars you'll miss out of your paycheck today can mean the difference between eating cat food or living easy-breezy on the Florida coast at age 60.

FLEXIBLE SPENDING ACCOUNT DEDUCTION

Although it's unlikely, you may be offered a Flexible Spending Account (FSAs) as a way to pay for health care. Through FSAs, money is deducted from your paycheck BEFORE TAXES, and put into a savings account. You can use this money to pay for health care or medical needs for yourself or for dependent care for an elderly parent. This is a great way to squirrel away money for medical expenses without worrying about taxes. But there's one big caveat—FSAs have a "use it or lose it" rule. You must spend the money on qualified expenses each year or lose the money you save.

HEALTH SAVINGS ACCOUNT DEDUCTION

Health savings accounts (HSAs) are a relatively new thing. Like FSAs, they allow you to deduct money from your paycheck BEFORE TAXES are applied and put it into a savings account for health-care expenses. Unlike FSAs , HSAs are owned by you, the individual, and not your employer. In addition, you won't lose any money that is left in the savings account at the end of the year. All your savings roll over to the next year. Still, you can only participate in an HSA if you have a high-deductible insurance plan and no other health coverage.

CHARITY DEDUCTION

As a service to the employee and the community, many employers allow their employees to contribute directly to one or more charitable organizations.

PART 3
BANKING 101

When you think about banks, you probably imagine a very simple process: you put your money into the bank and/or you take it out. The banking process is a lot more complicated than that, though. There are different types of banking institutions, but they do have some things in common, such as the use of interest and the need to follow federal rules and banking regulations. It's important to understand the basics of banking so that you can be a smart consumer, compare services, and watch out for fees.

In addition, you do lots of things online, so it shouldn't be a surprise that you can do your banking, pay your bills, and conduct other financial transactions via your computer. Online banking and bill paying is easy and convenient, but there are important issues (such as security concerns) that you need to know about—and we'll give you the essential info you need.

CHAPTER 4
MAKING CENTS OUT OF BANKING

You've probably heard stories about how people in the old days used to keep their money in their mattress. Well, people realized that's not really a good idea for a bunch of reasons (burglaries, fire, bed bugs, you name it). So now most people keep their money in banks. Banks also offer other services that can make your life easier, such as providing a debit card, giving loans, and helping you save for a goal or emergency fund.

HOW BANKS WORK

When depositing your money into a bank, the bank doesn't keep ALL of your money. Nope, in fact, the bank will turn around and lend some of your money—and money of its other customers—to other people, institutions, and even other banks. These lenders pay the bank a little extra for that loan service. This extra over the amount of the actual loan is called interest. The bank may even share the profit from its interest payments with you just for giving them your money to lend out.

But what happens when you go to the bank to withdraw your money? Well, the bank has millions of customers! It uses all of its assets to serve you and everyone else who needs cash.

So a bank is basically like a constant revolving door—the bank takes money in, while at the same time it is lending money out.

NOW THIS IS INTERESTING: UNDERSTANDING INTEREST RATES

Interest is what you earn by keeping your money in a bank. It is basically the fee the bank pays you for letting it keep (and use) your money. Interest works on a percentage basis. So, if the bank offers 4 percent interest, it will pay you 4 percent of whatever your balance is. If you deposit $100, you will earn 4 cents in interest after a certain period of time.

EXPERT ADVICE!

A bank is a business. In fact, it invests your money so that it can make more money of its own. In return, the bank pays you interest for the use of your cash, which is not much right now. The bank earns income by collecting money from businesses and people who want to keep their money in the bank. The bank lends this money to others and charges them interest for their loans.
~ *Ornella Grosz, Financial Literacy Advocate and Author of "Moneylicious: A Financial Clue for Generation Y"*

The interest rate a bank offers varies depending upon the economy. You can always ask an employee at your bank what the current interest rate is.

You might be amazed at how quickly your money can grow thanks to interest. This is partly due to a sort of magical power called Compound Interest (CI). Here's what that means: At the end of the first month, your account earns interest based on what you started out with (your initial deposit). You will then have a new balance—your deposit plus the added interest. Now, the next month, you will earn interest on that current amount. In other words, you will earn interest on your interest. (Got that?) For example, if you have a dollar and you get 4 cents interest, the bank will use $1.04 as the starting amount next time when calculating your interest. That's, of course, if you do not withdraw any money during the month. The beauty of CI can truly be realized when you start saving in retirement accounts. Let's say you start a retirement account today in your teens with $1,000. You decide to save $100 a month and receive an annual interest rate of 4 percent.

Before you reach age 40, your $1,000 + $100 a month investment will have grown to $39.354.17! That's the amazing power of CI.

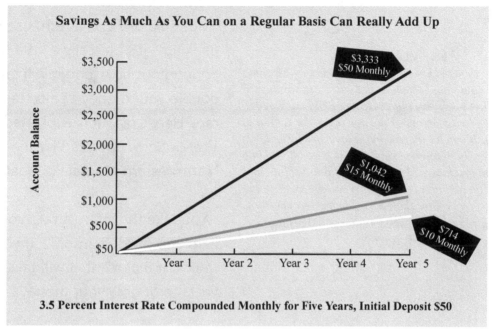

Savings As Much As You Can on a Regular Basis Can Really Add Up

3.5 Percent Interest Rate Compounded Monthly for Five Years, Initial Deposit $50

Source: FDIC Consumer News

For a hands-on look at how interest compounds, check out the Compounding Calculator at TheMint.org, developed by the Northwestern Mutual Foundation with the National Council on Economic Education (NCEE). TheMint.org is endorsed by the American Library Association. Visit: http://themint.org/kids/compounding-calculator.html.

72 REASONS TO LOVE BANKING

The "Rule of 72" is a term used in banking—it's basically a little trick for figuring out how long it will take you to double your money at a certain interest rate. Here's how it is explained on TheMint.org, operated by the Northwestern Mutual Foundation:

You take the interest rate you expect to earn and divide it into 72. If you expect a return of 6 percent, it will take twelve years to double your money.

Example: You are age 24 and have $3,000 in a savings account earning 8 percent annually. According to the Rule of 72, it will take nine years to double your money. At age 33, you will have $6,000 if you add nothing more to the account. At age 42, you will have $12,000. Then, at age 60, you'll have $48,000 from a $3,000 investment. Amazing isn't it? All you had to do was to leave your money alone, and it earned you $45,000 ($48,000 minus your original $3,000 investment) with no effort on your part! It's like magic.

HOW TO CHOOSE A BANK

There are a ton of banks out there—in some towns, it may seem like there's a bank on every block, especially when you count ATMs, drive-through branches, and bank locations in grocery stores.

So how do you pick the best bank for you? There are a few things you need to think about.

- **What account type are you looking for?** Do you want to just save the money you make? Then you're looking for a bank that offers a good interest rate on a savings account. On the other hand, if you want more liquidity to your bank account—meaning the ability to withdraw money when you need it—you want a bank that offers a NO-COST checking account. Banks often have several different types of checking and savings accounts, each with their own perks and fees. These days banks have fees for everything! They charge for opening accounts, for not having enough money in an account, for overdrawing the account (that's spending more money than you have in the account on a purchase), or even not using the account often enough. It's important to check out the fees attached to your potential account, as they can really add up.

- **What about location?** Does the bank have a lot of branches and/or ATMs in your area and areas where you go frequently? If you're in college or will be heading there soon, make sure you pick a bank that's available in that area.

- **Talk to your parents.** There may be perks for having an account at the same bank as your parents. You won't know until you ask.

Questions to ask:

- Do I need a minimum balance in my account?

- What fees are charged for this account?

- How many ATMs do you have, and where?

- What fees will I be charged for ATM or debit card transactions?

Be sure to ask about any special perks or accounts the bank may offer for students. Just make sure you also find out what happens when you graduate or otherwise are no longer a student. You don't want to walk across the stage with your diploma and suddenly start getting hit with a bunch of fees on your bank account.

BANK VS. CREDIT UNION

A credit union is another type of financial institution that is popular with many people. You must be a member of a credit union in order to be a customer. The rules of who can be a member vary, though it's often requires nothing more than depositing $5 into an account with the credit union. Some credit unions are for employees of a certain industry or company. Other credit unions are for anyone who can maintain an account. The credit union is run by a board of directors. The biggest difference between a bank and a credit union is that the members of the credit union own the financial institution as opposed to banks that are owned by large Wall Street Firms. Credit unions are popular with working people such as plumbers, teachers, and automobile workers.

Some people prefer credit unions because they tend to be smaller than banks and offer a more personal touch, unlike big banks where you are often dealing with what feels like a huge corporate machine.

Credit unions are becoming very common on college campuses and also offer some services that traditional banks do not. So, it may be worthwhile to check into some local credit unions in your area to see what they may be able to offer you. Credit unions are also excellent places to get low-cost loans for cars and other big purchases.

CHECK, PLEASE!

EXPERT ADVICE!

Jump$tart Coalition did a survey on financial literacy among high school students. According to this study, only 45% of the high school seniors surveyed had a checking account. Once they go off to college and are more or less on their own, they begin making mistakes. Of those college students surveyed, 30% admitted to bouncing a check.

~ Danny Kofke, special education teacher and author of "A Simple Book of Financial Wisdom: Teach Yourself (and Your Kids) How to Live Wealthy with Little Money" (Wyatt-MacKenzie, September 2011)

A checking account allows you to deposit money that you can then use to pay for bills, purchases, and other expenses by writing out a check. (Most people use few actual paper checks these days; instead, they use their checking account to pay bills online using electronic payments.)

Unlike a savings account, a checking account usually doesn't earn interest (although some banks are now offering interest-earning checking accounts—but there are often a lot of conditions you must meet in order to be eligible to earn interest with these accounts). So, if you want to stockpile money and let it grow, you would use a savings account. A checking account is mainly used to pay bills and expenses.

A checking account is an asset because it establishes a financial identity. It gives you credibility in the financial and professional worlds and means that you can both spend and receive money within an established banking system. When you're in high school, there's nothing wrong with operating on a cash-only basis, but that gets risky and cumbersome when you get older and your expenditures get more complex. A checkbook gives you credibility for not only employers, but rental agencies, car dealerships, and educational institutions.

READING YOUR BANK STATEMENT

Tales from a Real Teen

"I opened up a student account when I was 18 with a national bank. When I first had my account, there were no fees associated with my checking and savings account. However, when I graduated, I started having to pay close to $15 a month for my accounts and that can really add up over a year. You may also have to send your bank a current school transcript if you are in school for more than four years because most student accounts won't maintain their student status longer than that without proof that you are still in school."

~ Lindsay Long, Austin, Texas

Once you've found a bank or credit union and opened an account, you'll get a check book and/or an account savings book. In addition, most banks offer you the opportunity to do all of your banking online. You should keep careful track of how much money you earn and how much you spend by writing the amounts down in your check book or checking the transactions online. This is called keeping your account balanced.

Each month, you should receive get a bank statement. This statement is basically a log of all the activity for that account during the month. Use this as a way to reconcile your income and spending activity you've already logged in your checkbook or savings book. While banks traditionally send statements via postal mail, many banks now allow you to access your statements online—and even from your Smartphone.

It's important to read your statement carefully. For one thing, there's always the possibility that there is some type of mistake. But you also need to make sure you are aware of every transaction, so that you have an accurate picture of your account and know exactly what your available balance is. Otherwise, you could be charged fees for overdrawing your account.

THE TRUE PRICE OF BEING OVERDRAWN

When you write out a check that is more than the amount you have available in your account, this puts your account balance in the negative. This is called being overdrawn. Depending upon your bank's policies, it will either honor the check (leaving your account in negative balance; you will need to deposit enough to cover the shortfall), or it will return the check to the person who tried to cash it. This is called a bounced check.

TIP

If you write an amount that doesn't take up the entire "amount" line on the check, draw a line across the blank space, to prevent someone else from adjusting the amount.

Overdrawing your account is a huge bummer because it means that the account you wrote a check from had insufficient funds to cover the amount you said you were good for. Not only is this totally embarrassing, it also results in fees and charges that add up quickly. Banks charge anything from $30 to $40 for every overdrawn transactions. In addition, whoever you wrote the check to will also charge you at least $25 for the bounced check. On top of all this, YOU STILL OWE the amount of money you wrote the check for. It is very important that you are aware of every instance of spending: your balance is how much is in your account, not how much you would have left after all of your checks have cleared. If you check your balance and it's surprisingly (delightfully!) high, then be sure you're taking all of the checks you've written into account. It's not uncommon for young spenders to spend beyond their means because they simply are not remaining conscious of every cent they said they were good for.

Regardless of whether the bank honors the check or not, it will probably charge you an
overdraft fee. This can be as much as $40 or more. And it's important to note that this is
usually charged for each transaction. So, if you write out three checks that come in while
your account is overdrawn, you will be charged three separate overdraft fees. Needless
to say, these fees can really add up! Collectively, banks have made more than $30 billion
annually just on the $30–$40 fees they charge for each instance an account is overdrawn.
So be careful of how much you're spending each month. It could mean the difference
between having money in the bank and owing money to the bank!

PUTTING THINGS IN BALANCE

A sure way to keep your account from being overdrawn is to balance your checkbook. This
means making sure your total, after all the transactions for the month, matches the current
balance on your bank statement.

Here's an easy step-by-step guide to balancing your checkbook from Practical Money
Skills for Life at http://www.practicalmoneyskills.com/:

Step 1: Get a copy of your monthly bank statement. Remember, you receive them either via mail or online each month.

Step 2: Compare your statement to your checkbook register. Throughout the month, you should have been recording every deposit and purchase or withdrawal. If you see any charges or deposits on your statement that aren't in your register, add them.

Step 3: Record any fees or balance adjustments that may appear in your statement.

Step 4: Subtract from your register's balance any checks you have written but that have not yet cleared the banking system. Don't forget to also subtract your debit charges if you have a debit card! (Read more about debit cards later in this chapter!)

Step 5: Check to see if the total matches your statement. If it does, your account is balanced. If not, go back through your register and see if you've missed anything or if you've made a mistake with your math.

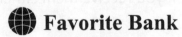

Favorite Bank

1000 Street Lane
Small Town, State 12345

Cynthia Customer
2468 Anywhere Drive.
Small Town, State 12345

Bank Statement   Primary Account Number: 001122334455

If you have any questions about your statement,	**Statement Date:**	**June 3, 2012**
Please call us at 555-555-5555	**Page Number:**	**1**

STUDENTCHECKING Account #001122334455

Summary Account #001122334455

Beginning Balance on May 2, 2012	$7,126.11
Deposits & Other Credits	+3,615.08
ATM Withdrawals & Debits	-689.02
Visa Check Card Purchases & Debits	-1,080.50
Withdrawals & Other Debits	-2,603.22
Checks Paid	-1,245.75
Ending Balance on June 3, 2012	**$5,122.70**

Deposits & Other Credits Account #001122334455

Description		Date Credited	Amount
Deposit	Ref No: 130012345	05-15	$3,615.08
Total Deposits & Other Credits			**$3,615.08**

ATM Withdrawals & Debits Account #001122334455

Description	Tran Date	Date Paid	Amount
ATM Withdrawal 1000 Street Lane Small Town, State 123458	05-19	05-19	**$20.00**

COMMON TERMS USED BY BANKS

Assets: Resources you own that have value, such as your iPod and Smartphone (if you're lucky).

ATM: Automated Teller Machine. It's a machine that gives you money from your account. Just remember that you need to deposit money in your account in order to take it out.

Balance: The amount of money in your bank account. Always pay close attention to what this is.

Bank: A place that stores money for later use.

Cash: Paper money and coins.

Check: A written promise that the bank will pay someone money. In the old days, it was written on an official piece of paper, but these days it's often an electronic transaction.

Credit: Buying on the promise that you will pay for it later.

Debit Card: A card linked to a bank account that is used to pay for purchases instead of cash or checks.

Deposit: Money put into an account.

Interest: Fee charged by the bank to use money.

Money: Currency used to exchange for goods and services.

Mortgage: A note with a promise to pay that's used to buy a house. (*Mortgage* is a French term meaning "death contract!")

PIN number: Personal Identification Number, which you use to access your account. Tip: This should not be 1234. You think nobody would ever guess that number, but trust us, somebody will.

Withdrawal: Money taken out of an account.

Farewell to the Float

Up until fairly recently, when you wanted to pay for something with money from your checking account, you wrote out a paper check and gave it to the store or whomever you were paying. The receiver of your check would then deposit it at his or her bank and wait for it to clear. The process usually took several days. So even if you didn't have enough money in your account to cover the check at the time you wrote it, you usually had a least a day or two in which you could make a deposit before the check would come in. This was often referred to as the "float" time.

These days, check processing is done electronically. In fact, at many stores, if you pay by check, the register actually scans the check and then the cashier returns it to you. That's because the register's computer is able to record the scanned information and electronically process the check. As a result, the money can be taken out of your account immediately. This means you can no longer enjoy the float.

PRACTICE MAKES PERFECT—FILLING OUT A CHECK

Even though so much of banking takes place online these days, there are those occasions when you still will need to fill out a check. If you've never done this before, don't worry. It's not hard at all. Here are some tips below, thanks to TheMint.org:

Jane & John Doe
555 Saveland Ave.
Acmeville, WI 54321

123

Date _____

PAY TO
THE ORDER OF _____ $ _____

_____ / 00 DOLLARS 🔒

THE MINT *SAVINGS & LOAN*

MEMO _____

⑂'001123451   ⑂'23 12 3456⑂' 123

1. Enter the DATE in the blank in the upper right corner. Include the month, the day, and the year. You can write out the date as January 4, 201X—or you can use all numbers 01/04/1X.

2. Write the name of the person or company you are paying on the "Pay to the order of," blank. Get the spelling right.

3. To the right of the "Pay to the order of," blank is a box with a dollar sign. Using numbers, write the amount in dollars and cents. Be sure to clearly place the decimal point between the dollar numerals and the cents numerals. For example: $32.15.

4. The next line is used to confirm the amount of the check, just in case the numbers are difficult to read in the dollar-sign box. In clear handwriting, write out the amount using words and fractions. Write out the dollar amount. Then add an "and," followed by the amount in cents written as a fraction. For example: Thirty-two dollars and 15/100. If you have any room left, draw a line to the end of the blank so no one can add to what you've written on that blank.

5. The Memo line in the lower left hand corner is a reminder line and can help you stay organized. For example, if you are buying a pair of jeans and are paying by check, you can write "jeans" on this line. If you write several checks to the same place, like a department store, this line helps you identify which check paid for jeans, which check paid for shoes, and which check was used for socks and a sweatshirt. If, however, you are paying a bill to the electric company or a department store, you may need to put your account number on this line.

6. The signature line, the line in the lower right corner of the check is where you write, not print, your name. Decide how you are going to sign your name, and then sign it the same way on all your checks. This is a formal document, so you probably want to sign it Andrew or Alexis rather than Andy or Lexi. Your bank will keep your signature on file as a way of verifying your signature on checks and other documents.

"The FDIC—that's short for Federal Deposit Insurance Corporation—is part of the U.S. government. The FDIC was created by Congress in 1933 after a terrible economic period called "The Great Depression" when thousands of banks shut down and families and businesses all across America lost money they had deposited in those banks. The FDIC's primary job is to make sure that, if a bank is closed, all of the bank's customers will get their deposits back—including any interest they've earned—up to the insurance limit under federal law. In the 70-plus years since the start of the FDIC, we have responded to about 3,000 bank failures, and we are proud to say that no depositor has lost a single penny of insured money."

~ Courtesy of FDIC Consumer News, http://www.fdic.gov

EXTRA INFO: At the bottom left corner of the check, you'll see some numbers. The first set is the **Routing Number.** This identifies the bank the check belongs to—each bank has a unique number. The next set of numbers is your account number followed by the number of the check you're writing, which should match the number in the upper right-hand corner.

BTW, You Can Use an ATM

When you have a bank account, you will often receive an ATM card (ATM is bank lingo for automated teller machine). An ATM card allows you to get your money from a machine 24/7, even if the bank is closed. You can also make deposits and do other banking at the ATM. In order to use your card at the ATM, you will need to enter your private security code or PIN number. Make sure you memorize your PIN, and don't tell it to anyone. If you share your PIN with another, you run the risk that this person will be able to get your money if he or she gets a hold of your ATM card.

Warning: Some ATMs charge you a fee to use an ATM that's not operated by the banking institution that issued you the card. These fees can range from $1 to $3 added on to the amount you withdraw. Often, the fees are issued by your bank as well as the bank of the ATM you are using if they're not one in the same.

DEBIT OR LEAVE IT

> **TIP**
>
> To impose a limit on how much you're going to spend in a set period of time—a night, a weekend, a trip to the mall—try just taking out a set amount of cash from the ATM and setting that as your limit. That way, once you're out of cash, you're done spending. This ensures not spending more than you're able to.

A debit card is like an ATM card with special powers. A debit card lets you make purchases at stores and online. The debit card will usually have a Visa or MasterCard logo on it, so it may look like a credit card. However, there is one important difference: When you pay for something with a debit card, the money is taken right out of your checking account. So, you need to make sure you have enough money in your account to pay for whatever it is you want to buy. Otherwise your transaction may be declined or your account might become overdrawn.

Some things to consider with debit cards:

• They often have daily spending or withdrawal limits. So if you try to buy something that is more than that limit, your transaction may be declined, even if you have more than enough money in
your account.

• The security protection rules may differ somewhat from credit cards. Be sure to review your bank's policies online so you know what risk you may face should someone make unauthorized charges or purchases with your card.

- There is more risk involved, in that if someone gets a hold of your card or your account numbers, the person can take money right out of your bank account. (Yes, the bank may credit that amount back if you file a fraud dispute, but that could take some time.)

- For certain transactions, a debit card may not be acceptable. For example, some car rental agencies will not accept debit cards.

CHAPTER 5
ONLINE BANKING AND BILL PAYING

You do pretty much everything else online, so why not manage your money online? Many banks offer online banking—and, in fact, they often encourage people to use it. It saves the bank the time and expense of sending out paper statements and allows you to do a lot of transactions yourself without having to bother a teller or other bank employee. It's more convenient for you because you can do your banking from the comfort of your own home, at any time of day or night. So it's a win-win for everyone!

ADVANTAGES OF ONLINE BANKING

Online banking offers some advantages when compared to going to an actual bank location to do your banking business. As we've already mentioned, it's very convenient. You can access your account online from wherever you are (as long as you have a secure Internet connection, of course). You can do your banking at any time, day or night, and you don't have to get in the car and drive anywhere, which saves you a lot of time. The transactions themselves are often done very quickly, as compared to standing in line at a bank and waiting for a teller.

Many people also find that it's easier to keep track of their banking transactions and balances when they use online banking, because all of their activity is recorded and available for review right there.

Also, if you use any sort of budgeting software program, it usually is designed to interact well with your online banking system.

DISADVANTAGES

There are a few drawbacks with online banking. First, obviously, you aren't dealing with an actual person, so you can't ask questions. (Although most online banking systems do allow you to submit a question or get help, and some even offer an instant chat service with an online teller!)

There may be some delay in when your transaction is processed or officially posted to your account. For example, transfers made after a certain time of day may not be posted until the next day. Be sure to check your bank's Web site for details as to processing times. Some people worry about security issues when banking online. We will discuss this more in this chapter.

DIRECT DEPOSIT

Direct deposit is when your paycheck or other payment is automatically deposited into your bank account. This is very convenient because you don't need to worry about picking up your paycheck (or waiting for it to arrive in the mail) and then going to the bank to deposit or cash it.

AUTOMATIC SAVINGS

If you want to help your savings grow without having to think about it too much, you can set up an automatic transfer. This is where a certain amount of money is automatically transferred from your checking account into a savings account on a specific date.

ONLINE-ONLY BANKS

Recently, there's been a trend of a new type of bank cropping up. These are online-only banks (also sometimes called virtual banks). As you can probably guess, these are banks that operate solely online and don't have any physical bank locations. If you already do most of your banking online and are comfortable banking in that way, a virtual bank may be a good option for you. Because these banks don't have the expenses of maintaining buildings, they may offer better interest rates and other perks.

ONLINE BILL PAYING

Forget the stamps and the envelopes—many banks offer you the opportunity to pay your bills electronically. Some banks allow you to enter the name and address of the place or person you want to pay and then that amount is automatically deducted from your account and sent to the recipient—namely through an electronic check. You may also be able to set up recurring automatic payments—say, if you want to pay a certain amount every month to that same place. Beware, some banks charge a monthly fee for this service!

In other cases, you may need to go to the Web site of the place you want to pay. Lots of places offer online bill pay these days, including utility companies, hospitals, and department stores.

Paying your bill online is easy. You just log into the site (after setting up an account) and enter your credit card or checking account information. Again, you can usually also set up automatic recurring payments or just make a one-time payment. For example, if you want to make sure your phone bill is paid every month without having to worry about it, you would set up a recurring payment so it is automatically taken from your bank account or charged to your credit card every month.

The advantage of online bill paying is that it is quick and easy. You don't need to worry about your payment getting lost or delayed in the mail, which could result in late charges. One thing to keep in mind, though, is that you must make sure the money is available in your account (or you risk overdraft charges and/or declined payments). This is especially true for automatic recurring payments. Be sure you know how much the bill will be, so you can make sure you have enough money in your account to cover it.

SAFETY FIRST

One big concern that is common when it comes to online banking is the issue of security. Generally, online banking is considered pretty safe. The major banking institutions spend a lot of money on security features and safeguards on their site to protect your information.

However, as with anything you do online, there is always the risk that something unexpected could happen. Even a few major retailers have had incidents where customer information was stolen or at least at risk.

Another issue is the possibility of a security flaw on your end, that is, if your computer has been infected with spyware or a virus that could allow someone else to view or record your banking activity (and other things you do online). Never conduct online banking transactions on public computer or a computer that anyone else but you has access to! Passwords and other information are often stored on computers even long after you've logged out of your account. When in doubt, don't bank online using public computers— it's just not worth the risk.

WATCH YOUR ACCOUNT ACTIVITY CLOSELY

It's important to keep a close eye on your bank accounts and debit/credit card accounts online (perhaps even getting in the habit of checking them on a daily basis). This way, you can quickly spot any signs that something may be wrong. Many banks offer alert services that send you text messages or e-mails when purchases over a certain amount are made or when your account balance dips below a set amount. Use these alert as a daily connection to your virtual money. When you access your account online, be sure to look for any purchases you didn't make or charges that don't look familiar to you. Don't overlook small charges—scam artists will often test the waters by making a small charge first, just to make sure the card is valid and working before attempting larger charges.

If you do spot something fishy, contact your bank or card company immediately. The company can cancel your card so that no other charges can be made. In most cases, you won't be responsible for any unauthorized charges made to your card as long as you notify your bank right away.

IDENTITY THEFT

Another security concern that you need to keep in mind is identity theft. This is when someone steals your personal information and uses it to open accounts in your name or use accounts you already have.

Identity theft can happen in lots of ways. Scammers may get a hold of your information online, or they can use an old-school tactic like going through your trash to find your account statements.

PROTECT YOURSELF

You can protect yourself by following these simple dos and don'ts, courtesy of Dollar Sensei (http://www.dollarsensei.com/TSAC/detectandprotect.htm#identitytheft_detect):

- **Don't** share your Social Security Number unless you have to. Keep your card in a safe place, but not in your wallet.

- **Don't** share your PIN number or computer passwords with anyone else. Memorize them, and do not write them down where others can see them.

- **Do** copy every credit or debit card that's in your wallet. That way, if they're lost or stolen, you'll have a record of who to call.

- **Do** follow the following ten steps for how to handle a lost or stolen wallet.

- **Don't** throw your statements and other financial information in the trash without shredding them first.

TEN WAYS TO PROTECT YOURSELF FROM FRAUD AND IDENTITY THEFT

To help prevent fraud and identity theft, Wells Fargo recommends these ten tips for young people:

1. Forward It: The Better Business Bureau recommends having sensitive mail sent to a permanent address such as a parent's home or a P.O. Box. This should include all financial and medical information, which may contain confidential details. Ask if a paperless statement is an option, so you can access account information online instead of by mail.

2. **Don't "Over Share" It:** Social media is increasingly popular, but it's a good idea to keep personal information private. Fraudsters can use personal information such as birth date, mother's maiden name, and pet's name, to help gain access to an account. Also, it's a good idea to keep other information such as mobile and home phone numbers; e-mail addresses; and dorm, apartment, and home addresses private.

3. **Doubt It:** Use a healthy dose of skepticism if someone claiming to be from your bank or another legitimate company calls, texts, or sends an e-mail asking for personal information. Never open unsolicited e-mails or links sent from strangers.

4. **Sign Up for It:** Consider signing up for online and mobile banking. This will enable you to monitor your accounts regularly, when it's convenient for you. Research has shown electronic banking is the quickest way to detect account fraud. Many financial service providers offer online and mobile banking.

5. **Ask for It:** Ask your financial services provider if it offers alerts, which can quickly detect unauthorized use of a bank account. Customized alerts can also be set up in advance. Alerts can be sent to an e-mail address or mobile device based on criteria you select. You can get alerts on almost anything related to your bank account, including when your bank balance drops below a certain amount or your credit card is charged more than a certain amount.

6. **Lock It:** Secure your laptop and desktop computer with a password, firewall, and anti-virus software, so no one else can access your files, and with a desktop cable lock, so no one can remove it. For your mobile devices, be sure to use the keypad lock or phone lock function when they are not in use. These functions password-protect your

device, so that no one else can use it to view your information. Also be sure to store your device in a secure location.

7. **Shred It:** Use a shredder and shred all unwanted credit card offers, insurance or loan applications, bills, credit card receipts, and documents that contain your personal information. Thieves steal information from many sources, including the mail and even garbage cans, and can use it to help gain access to financial accounts.

8. **Protect It:** Consider using a room safe, or secure online safe for copies of important documents. Be sure to keep any credit cards and documents that contain personal information—such as a passport, a Social Security Card, and your bank statements—locked up when not in use.

9. **Hide It:** Never leave a wallet or purse in plain sight. The same goes for documents with personal or account information.

10. **Learn More About It:** Ask your financial services provider what other services it offers to protect your personal and account information.

WATCH OUT FOR PHISHING AND ONLINE SCAMS

You must be careful and always have your guard up when you do almost anything online, but especially anything involving your money or personal information. There are a lot of scammers out there who are just waiting to get their hands on your account information. And they can be very clever in coming up with ways to get you to divulge this information.

One common tactic is phishing schemes. Phishing is when a scammer sends you an e-mail (or sets up a pop-up window that appears when you visit a Web site) that appears to be from a bank or other business you trust. The message will often warn that there's been a security breach with your account, and you must take action immediately or your account will be frozen. The actual story may change, but there is usually a sense of urgency, to try to get you to take action quickly before you have time to think about it.

You are instructed to click on a link that has been set up to appear as if it leads to a trusted Web site. You will then usually see a Web page that looks official—but is actually a fake copy of a real Web page. This fake page is created and controlled by the scam artist. The sole purpose is to get you to enter your login information and other account details, which the scam artists then records so he or she can get access to your account.

How to Avoid Getting "Hooked" by a Phishing Scam

The FTC (Federal Trade Commission) offers these tips to avoid becoming a victim of a phishing scam:

- **If you get an e-mail or pop-up message that asks for personal or financial information, do not reply.** And don't click on the link in the message, either. Legitimate companies don't ask for this information via e-mail. If you are concerned about your account, contact the organization mentioned in the e-mail using a telephone number you know to be genuine, or open a new Internet browser session and type in the company's correct Web address yourself. In any case, don't cut and paste the link from the message into your Internet browser—phishers can make links look like they go to one place, but actually send you to a different site.

- **Area codes can mislead.** Some scammers send an e-mail that appears to be from a legitimate business and ask you to call a phone number to update your account or access a "refund." Because they use Voice Over Internet Protocol (VOIP) technology, the area code you call does not reflect where the scammers really are. If you need to reach an organization you do business with, call the number on your financial statements or on the back of your credit card. In any case, delete random e-mails that ask you to confirm or divulge your financial information.

- **Use anti-virus and anti-spyware software, as well as a firewall, and update them all regularly.** Some phishing e-mails contain software that can harm your computer or track your activities on the Internet without your knowledge. Anti-virus software and a firewall can protect you from inadvertently accepting such unwanted files. Anti-virus software scans incoming communications for troublesome files. Look for antivirus software that recognizes current viruses as well as older ones, that can effectively reverse the damage, and that updates automatically.

- **A firewall helps make you invisible on the Internet and blocks all communications from unauthorized sources.** It's especially important to run a firewall if you have a broadband connection. Operating systems (like Windows or Linux) or browsers (like Internet Explorer or Netscape) also may offer free software "patches" to close holes in the system that hackers or phishers could exploit.

- **Don't e-mail personal or financial information.** E-mail is not a secure method of transmitting personal information. If you initiate a transaction and want to provide your personal or financial information through an organization's Web site, look for indicators that the site is secure, like a lock icon on the browser's status bar or a URL for a Web site that begins "https:" (the "s" stands for "secure"). Unfortunately, no indicator is foolproof; some phishers have forged security icons.

- **Review credit card and bank account statements as soon as you receive them to check for unauthorized charges.** If your statement is late by more than a couple of days, call your credit card company or bank to confirm your billing address and account balances.

- **Be cautious about opening any attachment or downloading any files from e-mails you receive, regardless of who sent them.** These files can contain viruses or other software that can weaken your computer's security.

- **Forward spam that is phishing for information to spam@uce.gov and to the company, bank, or organization impersonated in the phishing e-mail.** Most organizations have information on their Web sites about where to report problems.

- **If you believe you've been scammed, file your complaint at ftc.gov, and then visit the FTC's Identity Theft Web site at www.ftc.gov/idtheft.** Victims of phishing can become victims of identity theft.

KEEP AN EYE ON YOUR CREDIT REPORTS

People often don't even realize they've been the victim of identity theft until they apply for a loan or credit account and someone checks their credit—and suddenly something strange pops up on their credit report. This is why it's important to check your credit report regularly and watch closely for any accounts or activity you don't recognize. See Chapter 7 for more information about credit reports and how to check yours.

PART 4
BEING FINANCIALLY
RESPONSIBLE

Saving money isn't exciting, but it is smart. It's usually the only way you can purchase big ticket items. There are many ways to save, along with options of where you put your savings. We'll share some ways to make your savings grow quickly and tricks for making saving money easier.

CHAPTER 6
SAVING FOR A RAINY DAY

One great thing about making money is having the ability to buy and do what you want—or what you're earnings allow! But it's also important to try and save money for unexpected expenses—or even to save up for a bigger goal, such as buying a car or going on a vacation. Saving money isn't always easy, especially if your paycheck never seems to go far enough (even many adults have that problem!). But if you get into the saving habit, pretty soon you will start saving money without even missing it.

THE IMPORTANCE OF SAVINGS

Creating a savings fund is important for many reasons. Savings provide an emergency lifeline that can help you when, say, your car breaks down or with a major expense such as going to college! Most importantly, a savings fund takes the financial pressure off by providing money when you really and truly need it. If you learn to save now, you'll develop a habit of putting away money for a rainy day. This habit is smart financial thinking that will serve you well throughout your whole life. Plus, having your own money is the key to becoming independent and self-sufficient.

> **A Reminder of Some Important Terms**
> A **deposit** is money you put into a bank. When you take the money back out later, that's called a **withdrawal. Interest** is a fee paid for borrowing money. When you take out a loan, you usually have to repay the amount you borrowed plus interest. With a savings account, the bank pays you interest because it is basically using your money while holding it for you.

WHERE TO PUT YOUR SAVINGS

SAVINGS ACCOUNTS

When you were young, you may have had a piggy bank where you put extra change or your allowance. Now that you are older, you need a better place to stash your savings. Probably the best option is to open a savings account at a bank. This way, your money will earn interest while it's sitting there. See the section on earning interest in Chapter 4 for more information about that.

It's common to open a savings account along with a checking account, so you may want to open both types of accounts at the same time. You will use both of them, but in different ways. You should be putting money into both your checking and savings accounts regularly—if you have direct deposit, you can have a certain percentage disbursed to each—but you should only be spending from checking. A savings account is created for only one purpose—to SAVE. Whether you're saving up for a car, part of your education, or a new computer, you should not use your savings account the same way you use your checking account. Maybe a better way to think about your savings is as your own personal safety net. A savings account (with money in it) is a good thing to have should trouble ever arise. Meanwhile, the longer you keep it in there, the more interest you will earn.

INVESTMENT ACCOUNT

You may also want to put your savings into some sort of investment type of account, such as a money market or CD. These will allow you to earn interest, but the big catch is that you usually cannot withdraw or access your money for a certain period of time.

(However, that may be a good thing if you fear you may be tempted to spend your money if it is too easy to access.)

OPENING A SAVINGS ACCOUNT

It's very easy to open a savings account. You just go to the bank of your choice (be sure to bring along some ID) and tell them you'd like to open an account. You'll need to fill out some paperwork, and, depending on your age, your parents may also need to sign some papers.

In the past, when you opened a savings account, you would get a small booklet (called a "register") where you could keep track of your transactions—what you put in or took out of your account. This register has a long history dating back to the early 1800s. Before that time, only the bank registered money transactions—even those that occurred in personal accounts. But in the 1820s, banks introduced the "passbook," and it became the first time customers were able to record an official record of their account's transaction. In some circles, you'll still hear people refer to bank accounts as "passbook savings accounts." These days, banks really encourage you to do everything online. Some folks say there's really no need to write everything down in your little booklet because you can see your balance online; however, banks have been known to make mistakes. It's just good to keep your own record of expenses. Besides, keeping the register up-to-date helps with your math skills!

The **FDIC** (or Federal Deposit Insurance Corporation) is an agency of the federal government that insures your bank account, covering your deposits (up to $250,000). So even if something were to happen to the bank, you wouldn't lose your money.

HOW TO START SAVING

One way to start saving money is to make a budget. Determine your "must have," expenses. These include fixed costs such as your bus pass to get to school or your monthly subscription to the Internet. Then see what else you're spending your money on that you don't really need to have. These could include the latte you buy on the way to the bus stop. Take one item that isn't on your "must have" list, and cease to purchase it. Put that money into a savings account instead!

For example, if you have a latte habit, try going without for a while. Use the money you spend at Starbucks to put into your savings account. You probably didn't realize how much you were spending on coffee—but it will sink in once you have a nice stash of cash accumulated.

TAKE BABY STEPS

TIP

Use an online budgeting site like Mint.com that lets you track specific expenses, such as your coffee habit or your mall shopping excursions. You will be able to see exactly how much money you have spent on each thing so far this month or this year.

When you first start saving—especially if you have a large goal in mind—it can be tough to get motivated because it may feel like you'll never reach the finish line. The key is to start small and focus on little milestones—say, each paycheck you manage to sock away $25. Or you may simply want to set a goal of saving *something* every week, without the pressure of setting a specific dollar amount.

EXPERT ADVICE!

It may seem like your "future" is light years ahead, but it's never too early to start saving. Cutting back on one ordered pizza a week or a new sweater can help you put aside small amounts of money into a savings account. If you save just $10 a week throughout high school, you'll graduate more than $2,000 richer. That amounts to two years of books for college! .
~ Jackie Warrick, President & Chief
   Savings Officer at CouponCabin.com

If you were to put 50 cents every day into a jar, at the end of a month you'd have $15. At the end of a year, you'd have $180—that's like free coffee for three months, or the entire box set of your favorite TV show on DVD, or even a tablet computer. The key to saving small change, though, is to not dip into it. This is the beauty of a piggy bank—there's space to put the money in, but it's very difficult to get it out.

"When I was saving up for my first computer for college, I estimated that I would need about $1,000 for the one I wanted. I then divided up the number of weeks in the summer and knew how much I needed to put away each week to reach my goal. It was hard, and I did have to turn down doing things like going out to the movies with friends, but I was able to reach my goal with a little bit of discipline. I also do silly things to me remember to save. For example, I print out a picture of what I'm saving for and wrap my check card in it, so that every time I go to buy something I see my savings goal and think hard about the purchase I am about to make."

~ Lindsay Long, Austin, Texas

GET YOUR FAMILY (OR FRIENDS) INVOLVED

Just like getting in shape, saving can sometimes be easier if you aren't doing it alone. Try getting your family involved. Come up with a way that all of you can save. You may even want to make it into a friendly competition—see who can save the most during a certain period. (Because your family members will probably have a wide range of incomes and available money, you may need to do this based on a weighted scale or a percentage of total income.) Or you can enlist friends to be your "saving buddies." To get them on board, remind them of something they'd really like to have but can't afford right now—this can be their goal of what they can splurge on, once their savings reach a certain amount.

SAVE IT BEFORE YOU SEE IT

If your pay is direct deposited, your bank may offer an "automatic savings" option where a certain portion of your paycheck is automatically routed into a savings account. If not, look into any other options that may allow you to stash part of your pay before you get the money in your hands.

KEEP (AND STASH) THE CHANGE

Here's a trick that will help you save change, which can then add up quickly. Whenever you pay for something with a bill—whether it's a dollar, five dollars, or whatever—take the change you get back and put it in a certain pocket. When you get home, put that change in a can or change jar, and deposit it in the bank once a week. You'll be surprised at how quickly it adds up! Tip: Some banks also allow you to do a similar action when you purchase items with your debit card—the bank will "round up" the amount and put the difference in your savings account.

CUT EXPENSES TO SAVE MONEY

The less money you spend, the more money you can save. So by cutting your expenses, you can easily add to your savings painlessly without even noticing any difference. Later in this book, we will talk about budgeting and tricks that can help you spend less.

> *Start small and simple, and learn to automatically put aside a small chunk of allowance every month. Even if it's just $5 a month, the idea is to learn to save a little on the side every time you get your hands on money. Open up an online bank account, like one at SmartyPig or Ally Bank, so you can earn interest on your savings. Earning interest is like earning a little bit more money just for having money safely saved in the bank. Once you get a part-time job and earn more money, put a little bit extra towards your savings to help your money grow more. Save every month and save automatically, and you'll find yourself with a nice nest of money (and an awesome financial habit) once you hit your 20s.*
> **~ Justine Rivero, Credit Advisor at CreditKarma.com**

CHAPTER 7
DON'T SPEND IT ALL IN ONE PLACE: CREATING (AND STICKING TO) A BUDGET

Probably the most important thing you need to do when it comes to managing your money is creating a budget. For most people, creating a budget isn't so hard—but sticking to it can be a challenge.

A budget is where you track what money you have coming in, and then plan where it will go. Having a budget is important because otherwise it's easy to spend all of your money on non-essentials—and, before you know it, you have no money left, and you still haven't paid your bills or taken care of important expenses.

BUDGETS AND INFLATION

When you're creating a budget you become increasingly aware how much products cost. Suddenly, you are paying attention to how much you pay for a Snickers® bar on a weekly basis. You also start to notice the instant the price changes. Any increase affects your budget. What you're becoming aware of is a mysterious economic term that affects everyone, including teens, but few really understand. The official term is called "inflation," but more than its definition, inflation's very existence affects just how much money you'll have to budget each year for basic necessities such as food, gas, and even milk!

Though you do not need to thoroughly understand inflation—there are economists who still wrestle with its true meaning—it's good to get a cursory understanding of how inflation works so you can adjust your budget when necessary. First, the definition:

Inflation is the rate at which the price of goods and services rises. Example: If the inflation rate is 3 percent, then something that costs you a dollar today would cost you $1.03 a year from now.

A certain amount of inflation is evitable—the cost to make goods is expected to go up—but when the cost of goods rises too fast—faster than the amount of money people earn each year—and people can't afford to buy needed items, then inflation has a negative side effect. Those rich enough to buy goods may buy as much as possible, while those too poor may have to go without. Such a run on goods can lead to dire consequences, such as widespread poverty, homelessness, and even war. This often happens in developing countries, for example the inflation crisis in Brazil in the 1980s, but it also occurred in Germany in the 1920s just before World War II.

For you, inflation means your money won't stretch as far as it previously did. If you make $100 a week now, you won't be able to buy as much as you did a year or two ago with that same weekly salary. So as inflation increases, the amount of goods you can buy decreases. (If you are really lucky, you will have a job where your annual raise is roughly the same as—or more than—the rate of inflation, but that's pretty rare these days.)

INFLATION AND BUYING POWER

When talking about inflation, the term "buying power" is sometimes used to describe how much a certain amount of money would be worth in today's economy—or what you could buy with that amount. For example, $100 in 1990 is the equivalent of $175.78 today, adjusted for inflation. So, the two amounts have the same buying power.

Inflation and its relation to rising prices or the value of money can be challenging to try to really understand, because in many cases it doesn't seem to follow a formula.

Let's take a look at how some prices today compare with those from 1990.

1990 PRICES

A gallon of gas cost an average of $1.34 in 1990. Adjusted for inflation, it should cost $2.35 now. If you've put gas in a car lately—or heard someone else complain about the cost of filling up—you know that gas costs way more than that, so the prices have been rising much faster than the rate of inflation.

The average cost of a new car in 1990 was $16,000. If you adjust that for inflation, you have a price of $28,125 today.

(By the way, in 1990, an IBM PS1 desktop computer—which saved files on storage devices called floppy disks—cost between $999 and $1,999.)

You may have heard the expression "not keeping up with inflation." People often say this when talking about how their pay has not increased enough to keep up with the rising cost of living due to inflation.

A good tool to see what kind of "buying power" a certain amount of money in a given year would have today is the CPI (Consumer Price Index) Inflation calculator at http://data. bls.gov/cgi-bin/cpicalc.pl.

HOW TO SET UP A BUDGET

There are lots of ways to set up a budget. You can use a site like Mint.com that lets you organize a budget online. You can create a spreadsheet in Excel and keep it on your computer. You can get a fancy budgeting ledger from an office supply store. Or you can just write up a simple chart in a notebook.

It doesn't really matter so much what your budget looks like. The important thing is that you come up with a system you like and that's easy for you to keep current. Otherwise, you will quickly give up, and your budget will be long forgotten.

MONTHLY BUDGET WORKSHEET

	Week 1	Week 2	Week 3	Week 4	Week 5	TOTAL
Entertainment						
Transportation						
Food						
Clothes						
Gifts						

	Week 1	Week 2	Week 3	Week 4	Week 5	TOTAL
Cell Phone						
Personal Care						
Other						
Savings for Big Picture Items						
WEEKLY TOTALS						
					MONTHLY TOTAL=	

Did You Know?

Only nine states actually require that personal financial education courses be offered to students. No wonder so many teens don't know as much as they should about managing money!

When setting up your budget, first list your income for the month. Include all sources of income (job, allowance, and anything else). If your income varies from month to month, it's usually a smart idea to estimate on the low end, just to be on the safe side. Next, make a list of all of your expenses. Start with the most important ones first—such as your cell phone bill, car insurance (if you have it), any school expenses, and other necessities. After that, you can list "luxuries" like clothes and entertainment. By setting a specific amount for these "luxury activities," in your budget, you might find it easier to decide which purchases are most important. (For example, if you have $50 for clothes in your budget, you may decide that spending $45 on a single shirt isn't a smart strategy.)

If possible, you should try to include savings in your budget. Even if you can only save a small amount, that's still better than nothing.

THE BEST LAID PLANS

EXPERT ADVICE!
"Save more than you spend. Ok, ok, I know what you are thinking, 'I am a teenager. I am working to play, to shop, and to have fun.' So true, but think about this: If you pay yourself first (instantly putting money into your savings), that money will grow, and that reward down the road will be greater and you will have something to show for all your hard work.".
~ Bethany Myers, MBA, Owner/Career Consulting at BLM Consulting

To plan your budget, consider your spending habits. Where does your money usually go? Don't be surprised if you don't know—at least, not exactly. Many people find themselves struggling to figure out how they spent all of their money without realizing it.

HOW FAR WOULD $100 GO?

How far can you stretch a buck? (Or $100?) That depends a lot on your spending (or saving) habits—and your shopping savvy.

Let's look at a few typical spending personalities, and see how far $100 would last them.

THE FASHIONISTA

You see a designer pair of boots at the mall. You tend to have no willpower when it comes to shopping (especially when it comes to boots), so you immediately reach for your wallet. The boots cost $125. Unless you can get a special discount or borrow some money from a friend, you only have enough for one boot and half of the other one. No matter, because if you don't buy the boots, you will surely see something else at one of the other stores that catches your eye. Your money won't even last an hour because it will be gone before you leave the mall.

THE "HEY, WHERE DID ALL MY MONEY GO?" SPENDER

This past week, you stopped for a caramel latte (cost: $4 each) every morning. You took a cab across town twice, at a cost of $5 each time. Yesterday, you grabbed a copy of People magazine ($4.99) and a container of Orbit gum ($2.50). You've downloaded twelve songs from iTunes® this week, at $0.99 each. You went to the movies with friends, where you had popcorn, a soda, and a box of Milk Duds (total cost, including the ticket: $23). One night, you had a craving for some junk food, and since the supermarket was already closed, you had to go to the convenience store, where they charged you $5 for a bag of Combos, $3 for a soda, and $2 for a candy bar. Now your cell phone bill is due, but you realize you've got less than $20 left, and you can't figure out where your money went because you really have nothing to show for it.

THE THRIFTY SAVER

You like to put as much of your cash into your savings fund as you can. You try to stick to a strict $20 weekly budget for "spending money." You buy snacks at the grocery store, and you pick generic brands whenever possible. You also aren't embarrassed to use coupons. You take the bus, walk, or carpool with friends. Instead of expensive nights out, you host get-togethers with friends at your house. You watch movies online or rent them through Netflix. For you, $100 would be more than enough for the week, and you'd have some to stash in your savings.

KEEP A MONEY DIARY

To really get a handle on how you spend your money, you may need to keep a "money diary" for several weeks. During this period, write down everything you spend—that means every single penny. Keep a tiny notebook with you, and jot down every purchase you make. Don't skip anything—even the 50 cents you spend on bus fare should be recorded.

EXPERT ADVICE!
"Budgeting is always a sensitive subject and requires a lot of conviction to successfully execute. An easier alternative is to pull out the same amount of money from an ATM each week, say $50, and allow that amount for your discretionary spending for the week. This way, you can physically see how much remains in your wallet, which makes it easier to plan your daily activities according to how much money you still have."
~ Gabe Albarian, President,
Financial Swagger, Inc.

At the end of the month, add up everything you recorded in your money diary. You can separate it by categories (or specific stores or bills). To get a really clear picture of your spending, put your list on an Excel spreadsheet, and create a pie chart or other colorful graphic in which you break down your spending by categories. You may be shocked to see what your biggest "money grabbers" are.

Pinpoint Your Priorities

EXPERT ADVICE!
"Write down EVERYTHING you spend money on for an entire month, from a $1 soda to a $25 haircut. This is an eye opener when it comes to wasting money! Just one Starbucks per day can add up to $100 a month! A better alternative might be to use the coffee pot! Maybe you will realize that you'd rather pack a lunch instead of buying lunch each day."
~ Kristl Story of TheBudgetDiet.com

An important part of planning your budget is determining your priorities and identifying your commitments. If you have payments, such as for a cell phone or other utilities, credit cards, or a loan, that should be an important priority. These are important commitments and should be at the top of your budget. If you have a tendency to want to splurge on shopping sprees, make sure you pay these bills immediately as soon as you get paid, before you have a chance to get distracted by the big sale at the mall. (Consider setting up an automatic payment arrangement via online banking, so the bills will be paid before you ever get the money in your hands.)

MAKE IT A FAMILY AFFAIR

Teens aren't the only ones who often find budgeting to be a challenge. Many adults have trouble tracking their spending and managing their budgets. So this may be a good opportunity to do a family activity together. Recruit your parents and siblings to join in, and together you can work on creating a family budget. You may even be able to teach your parents a few tricks, such as how to organize and track their expenses online.

NEEDS VS. WANTS

One of the toughest parts about budgeting your money and cutting back on expenses is determining your necessities—what you truly need. The basic rule of smart money management, especially when you need to live on a tight budget, is that you need to focus on what you need, not necessarily what you want. Again, this comes back to priorities. But it also requires you to be really honest with yourself about what you really need. Let's face it, that new iPhone case probably isn't something you really need. On the other hand, food is a necessity. Likewise, bus fare or a subway card may be a necessity if you need transportation to get to work.

Yes, it's not always fun to separate needs from wants. Almost always, the "wants" are more fun, while the needs tend to be the boring, practical stuff like food and shelter. Ideally, you will be able to squeeze room in your budget for a few fun things. (Later in this chapter are tips on saving money that may help you stretch your budget.) But if not, you need to make sure you take care of the necessities first.

COMMON EXPENSES—THE STUFF WE ALL WANT

There are some common areas where many teens spend a lot of their money. Again, how high these should be on your priority list depends on what other expenses you have and how much room you have in your budget.

GO-GO GADGETS!

This is an increasingly big expense for teens. While most teens today don't spend a lot of money on CDs these days, they do spend a lot on gadgets like gaming systems, phones, MP3 players, and other electronics and accessories.

> According to a survey by *Seventeen* magazine, 75 percent of teens would choose a new pair of shoes over 50 new MP3 downloads, and 63 percent would choose a new pair of jeans over tickets to a concert.

Fun Fact:

In 2009, 76 percent of all 8- to 18-year-olds owned an iPod or an MP3 Player.

This is the kind of thing you may want to start a savings fund for, putting away a certain amount each week until you can afford to buy it. It's also important to take good care of your electronics, so they can last as long as possible. Consider buying a replacement plan, especially if you tend to be rough on electronics.

CAN YOU HEAR ME NOW? CELL PHONE EXPENSES

Shocking Stat

In 2009, a 13-year-old from California racked up a whopping cell phone bill of more than $21,000 after downloading 1.5 kilobytes of data with his phone. That same year, a 13-year-old girl from Wyoming got a cell phone bill for nearly $5,000 after sending more than 10,000 text messages in one month.

Is a cell phone a necessity or a luxury? This is one thing you can probably debate, but you could make a decent case for listing it as a necessity. For safety reasons, it's a good idea to have a cell phone in case of emergencies, such as if your car breaks down or you have a problem while walking home late at night.

Most teens today do have a cell phone—not only do they have to pay for the phone, they also have a monthly bill. If you're lucky, your parents can add you to their family plan, which may make your individual bill lower than if you had an individual plan. Do your parents insist that you pay for your share of the bill? If so, you need to educate yourself about your phone plan, including rates and charges. Pay particular attention to monthly limits on minutes and text messages. Also find out about downloading rates and limits, especially if you access the Web a lot on your phone.

To keep your cell expenses under control and to make it easier to budget, consider going the prepaid route. There are several different carriers that offer prepaid plans, and you can choose from a bunch of different types of phones, including the PDA and flip-phone varieties. Some prepaid plans offer unlimited text and data options.

With a prepaid plan, you can buy a "minutes card" (available at major stores) that allows you to upload a certain dollar amount or level of minutes to your phone. Once you use up that amount, you need to get another card to add minutes. You may also be able to buy more minutes online. Most of the prepaid services allow you to register a credit card online, so your minutes will automatically be replenished when you run low, and you don't risk getting cut off.

Some services also have a monthly prepaid plan. Yes, you will have a monthly bill, but you don't need to worry about extra charges—and you don't have a contract or have to pass a credit check.

FOOD

Food and entertainment are big expenses for many teens. If you are buying your own groceries, then this would go under the "necessity" category. But for most teens, food purchases are in the form of fast food, lattes, and a bite to eat with friends after school. This is one of those areas where "little" expenses can add up quickly. That slice of pizza and soda may not seem like a big deal budget-wise, but if this is part of your daily routine, it can add up to a sizeable expense on a monthly basis.

> ## TIP
> Even if you don't actually have a current service plan—or if you've run out of minutes on your prepaid plan—keep your phone charged and with you. Most phones can still be used to call 911, regardless of whether you have any available minutes on your plan.

Cutting down on food purchases may be one of the quickest ways to drop expenses, but it might not be an easy adjustment, especially if this is part of your social routine. It may be easier if you can get your friends on board. Try to come up with creative alternatives—like maybe coming up with fun menus of things you can make at home. Then take turns hosting get-togethers at each other's houses. Potlucks can be fun!

Also, check out the Web sites of local restaurants to see if they offer online specials or deals on certain days of the week.

BORED TO DEATH, EXCITED TO DEBT

Entertainment often doesn't come cheap. But let's face it: It's hard to justify this as a necessity—although we know you will probably try! So if you're on a tight budget, this is probably the first place where you need to cut spending. If money is really scarce, you may need to cut entertainment expenses down to zero or close to it. That doesn't mean you can't have any fun, it just means you will need to be creative about coming up with free or cheap fun things to do.

If you do have a little bit of room for entertainment in your budget, this is a good time to flex your savvy shopping muscles. Use a service like Netflix (for movies) and GameFly (for video games) that lets you pay one flat fee each month. That makes it easy to plan the cost into your budget. And don't overlook your local public library—in addition to books, they often have DVDs that you can check out for free.

For concerts and shows, check out sites like StubHub to buy tickets. And be sure to look on the venue's Web site to see if they have any special deals on cheap tickets. Also, check online for "Free Things to Do" listings, as most major cities or even rural towns offer free festivals, concerts, and even food fairs.

I GET AROUND: GAS AND TRANSPORTATION COSTS

Depending on where you live and your daily routine, you may have some transportation expenses, especially if you need a ride to work or school. If you have your own car, you will have costs of insurance, registration, and other expenses, unless your parents cover those costs. Then there is gas, which, at today's prices, can really become a major expense if you drive a lot.

> **TIP**
>
> Use online "deal hunter" forums, such as the ones at FatWallet.com, to get tips from other bargain hunters as to how to get the best deals. You can get great scoops on deals on just about everything, from electronics to clothing.

But even if you don't have a car of your own, you may have transportation costs, such as for public transportation. (Keep in mind that public transportation is earth-friendly and is often the fastest way to get around town. Plus, there are no parking hassles!)

If a friend or sibling gives you a ride frequently, you should offer to contribute some money toward the cost of gas.

CLOTHING

Even if you aren't a fashionista, clothing can still get expensive. If you attend a school with a dress code, you may essentially have two separate wardrobes—one for school and one for the rest of the time.

This is another case where it can really pay off to be a smart shopper. Watch for sales, and visit stores' Web sites where they often have special online deals. And sign up for the e-mail mailing list, if they have one, as you may get alerts about secret deals and maybe even receive coupons.

EXPERT ADVICE!
"Explore the world of discounted gift cards—the new way to save money! Save up to 35% on clothing, restaurants, movies, and more! Check out PlasticJungle.com."
~ Kristl Story of TheBudgetDiet.com

Kristl Story of TheBudgetDiet.com recommends checking out consignment shops, thrift stores, and stores like Plato's Closet that offer brand name, gently used clothing for great deals on trendy styles. You can often find items here for a fraction of what you would pay at a mall store. And while you're there, bring in some of your old clothes to sell or trade.

Vintage looks are really popular right now, so you may be able to find some of your favorite past fashion trends at thrift stores. Use your creativity and be original—you just may start some new trends! When in doubt, raid your parents' closets—you'd be surprised at how in style your mom's 1960s mini-skirt is.

WAYS TO SAVE MONEY AND CUT EXPENSES

In challenging economic times, teens are realizing it's important to be a savvy shopper (and saver). In a *Seventeen* magazine survey, 55 percent of teens say they are waiting for items to go on sale, 50 percent are making fewer "impulse purchases," and 42 percent are more likely to "comparison shop for the best price." Only 22 percent said that the economy has "little to no affect" on their shopping behaviors.

Unless you have an ATM in your bedroom, you only have so much cash to go around. The best way to stretch your budget (and make room for fun stuff) is to cut expenses and use smart strategies to save money wherever you can.

Many teens feel a little embarrassed (at least at first) about doing things like comparing sale ads and cutting coupons. But that embarrassment will quickly fade when you realize how much money you can save. Your friends may even be amazed when they see how far you can stretch your cash!

THREE THINGS YOU CAN DO TO MAKE YOUR MONEY LAST

By Tori Molnar, Teenage President and CEO of Utoria, and Founder of She Can Make Change www.myutoria.com

1. **Exchange extra effort to save money.** For example, instead of shopping at your leisure, try shopping during special events and holidays. There will be more people in the stores, but the deals are worth it! Many times, stores will offer up to 50 percent off during events like Black Friday, Labor Day, Memorial Day, Post-Christmas Clearance sales, and Back to School. People are often enraged by the extreme commercialization of holidays, but you should embrace it, and use the deals to your advantage.

2. **Trade in old things for money.** Instead of letting old clothes, shoes, and phones sit in the back of your closet, take your items to a consignment shop or sell them online. Doing this lowers the cost of the item to you, so in a sense, you just saved more money! For example, say you followed tip #1 and shopped during a sale and got a shirt that is regularly $29.99 for $15. You wear your shirt a few times and grow tired of it. You then take this shirt to the consignment sale, and they give you $8 for a shirt that you've already worn and enjoyed. Technically, this means that the $30 shirt you bought only cost you $7. That's a lot of money saved!

3. Look for coupons and special promotions before going out with friends. It's easy to wait to buy clothes, books, and electronics during special promotions, but you can't wait to have fun! So before you go to the movies, bowling, or to your favorite restaurant, look for coupons or go on a certain night when they're having a special promotion. This is a great idea if you are willing to compromise on what day you go out. Sometimes, you can also find comparable places that differ in price. For example, you may want to go to Subway®, but you have a "free sub" coupon for a comparable hoagie shop. Also, remember to try Google for coupons. For example, if you want to go to Fox's Pizza, just Google "Fox's Pizza coupons." This tends to have a pretty high success rate. You can also get subscription lists for coupons from your favorite restaurants. This provides coupons that come directly to you, rather than you having to go look for them. Now that's an easy way to save!

PART 5
CREDIT CARDS AND DEBT

Raise your hands if you love debt! Yeah, didn't think so. But with prices the way they are it's tough to avoid debt—especially if you want to buy a car or a house. Debt is fine if you can manage it responsibly. You also need to know how to monitor your own credit and what lenders (and others) look for when checking your credit. We'll share essential tips and information you need to know about paying with plastic to help you avoid getting into debt.

CHAPTER 8
UNDERSTANDING DEBT AND CREDIT

So you understand how money works, you've gotten a taste of how to earn it and can decipher your paychecks; you've even created a budget and a savings plan. But you know there's something else out there that you need to know about it. You see it in television commercials—car dealers offering brand new cars for "No Money Down!" People who couldn't even buy you lunch last week are buying brand new sneakers at $400 a pop. What gives? Well, most likely, those folks who are buying major purchases such as cars, houses, and even the new Michael Jordan's are using a magical key called **credit**. While it's ideal to open up a savings account and squirrel away money each week for that big purchase our economy doesn't work like that. We live in a consumerism economy and in order for us to buy all those products that keep factories, stores and most Americans employed, we use credit and debt—for good or ill!

WHAT IS DEBT?

For more than 5,000 years, those with items of value have been lending them to those in need. When you borrow value that you do not have, it is called debt. Nobody likes debt (something owed), but few people can manage to totally avoid it. If you ever want to buy a house or a new car, you will most likely need to get a loan—DEBT! In addition, many people use student loans in order to pay for college—DEBT! And finally, of course, there are credit cards—most people have several of those—DEBT—lots more debt! Today, most people rarely think that spending more than you earn is a problem. When the nation is in debt to the tune of $14 trillion—well, it's hard to take incurring debt or the idea that it needs to be repaid seriously. But in the 1800s, the jails in the United States were filled with debtors. People who owed as little as 50 cents were thrown into jail and often died there. Whew! It's a good thing that doesn't happen today. Still, if you borrow money and promise to pay it back, then make sure you keep that promise—it's your duty to do so!

WHAT IS CREDIT?

Credit is your ability to buy something even though you don't have enough money to pay for it upfront. You get a loan or a credit card and agree to repay that money (plus interest and other charges). This is a debt that you must pay back. Sometimes, especially if the debt is for a high amount, the lender requires collateral, which is property that the lender can take if you don't pay back the loan. For a mortgage, that would be the house, and for a car loan, it would be the vehicle. This is known as secured debt because the lenders have some security to ensure that they will get their money.

GOOD AND BAD CREDIT

If you have paid all of your bills on time and haven't racked up sky-high credit card bills, you probably have good credit. Good credit means you have a history of handling credit responsibly. On the other hand, if you've been late paying bills and have maxed out your credit cards, your credit may not be so good. Good credit is important because it makes it easier for you to get a loan. You will also usually get the best interest rate and terms if you have good credit.

Revolving credit is a credit account that you can use over and over again. For example, if you have a credit card and you pay off the balance, you can then use that available credit again to charge more purchases. Credit that you get for a mortgage or car purchase is usually an installment loan, where you borrow a specific amount and then pay a certain payment every month until the debt is paid off.

CREDIT REPORTING AGENCIES

A credit reporting agency (also known as a credit bureau) does not actually give loans or otherwise provide you with credit. But these agencies play an important role in your life when it comes to finances. They keep track of your credit history and credit-related transactions. They then use that information to compile your credit report and calculate your credit score. Your credit "worthiness" is judged mainly based on your credit reports and your credit score. There are three major credit reporting agencies: Equifax, Experian, and TransUnion.

CONTACTING THE CREDIT BUREAUS

Equifax

Phone: 800-685-1111 (toll-free)

www.equifax.com

Experian

Phone: 888-397-3742 (toll-free)

www.experian.com

TransUnion

Phone: 877-322-8228 (toll-free)

www.transunion.com

YOUR CREDIT REPORT

Your credit report is sort of like that notorious "permanent record" they always talk about in high school. The credit report is a detailed history of everything you've done in the past decade or so with regard to credit and finances. It includes information on your loans and credit cards. Just as your high school transcripts provide a good overview of what you did in high school, lenders (and others) can get a good idea of what you've done with your money by looking at your credit report. Each credit bureau differs in the information it gathers, so your report can look different from one bureau to another.

YOUR CREDIT SCORE

Often, lenders don't want to bother looking through your entire credit report, so there's a shortcut. Your credit report is "summed up" in the form of your credit score. Your credit scores are also known as your FICO scores. Just as colleges often judge you (at least in part) based on your SAT scores, lenders judge you based on your credit scores.

As we said before, each credit bureau collects different information, so your score can vary from one agency to another. Named after the first company to create a credit rating score, your FICO Scores can range from 300 to 850.

EXPERT ADVICE!

"The most important tip for teens right now is to have them pull their credit report at least six months or more before their 18th birthday. Too many kids are victims of identity theft, especially in this economy! Perhaps an adult put utilities or phone bills in a child's name because they were struggling to pay the mortgage or other bills, etc.

Teens need to pull their credit reports long before their 18th birthday because once they turn 18, the debt is theirs, and it is difficult to have it removed. Prior to their 18th birthday, they are minors, and it's much easier to have these debts removed. When teens pull their credit reports, it should state something along the lines of "no report found."

Many kids learn they've been victimized when they apply for a job, an apartment, and/or a car loan. By that time, they are over the age of 18 and strapped with debt that isn't theirs. About two thirds of employers check credit as part of the employment screening process. Although the laws are scheduled to end that practice, employers will still be able to pull credit for jobs that involve finance, money, security, and other areas."

~ Jennifer Matthews, MBA, Creating Financial Literacy, LLC,
   www.CreatingFinancialLiteracyLLC.com

There are five things that are considered when calculating your credit score:

1. **Payment history (weighted 35%):** Have you paid your bills on time? Have any of your accounts been late? If so, for how long?

2. **Amount You Owe (30%):** What is your total debt? How much of your available credit are you using? (In other words, are your cards maxed out?)

3. **Length of Credit History (15%):** How long have you had your accounts? Lenders like to see a long record of good payment habits, so the longer your history, the better.

4. **New Credit (10%):** How many times have you requested credit or opened new accounts recently? Lenders sometimes get nervous if they see you have taken out a bunch of credit all at once because they think you may take on too much debt that you won't be able to pay back.

5. **Type of Credit (10%):** It's good to have a mix of credit types: credit cards issued by a bank, department store credit cards, home equity lines of credit, installments loans, etc.

CHECKING OUT YOUR CREDIT REPORT

It's important to check out your own credit report so you know exactly what sort of shape your credit is in, and also so you can look for any errors. A lot of credit reports do contain errors and also frequently contain signs of identity theft or fraud.

It's never too early to start monitoring your credit. Even if you've never had a loan or credit card, it's still a good idea to check your credit report, just in case there's a problem (see Expert Advice below).

By law, you are entitled to get one free copy of your credit report per year from each of the three credit bureaus. The official site where you can request your free reports is AnnualCreditReport.com. There are many other sites that promise "free credit reports" but then will try to sign you up for costly monthly monitoring plan or other services. Be careful.

HOW BAD CREDIT CAN HURT YOU

Bad credit can cause you problems in many ways. For one, it will make it harder for you to get a loan or other credit. And if you do get credit, you will probably pay a higher interest rate than someone with good credit.

Bad credit can also make it tougher for you to get a job or rent an apartment. As you'll see later in this chapter, it isn't just lenders who may check your credit.

HOW IS YOUR CREDIT SCORE USED?

Your credit score is used to make decisions about your credit worthiness. So, lenders check your credit score before deciding whether to approve you for a loan or credit account.

However, there are other people who might be checking your credit report, as well.

LANDLORDS

Landlords check credit reports to help weed out deadbeat tenants. If you are trying to rent an apartment, the landlord may check your credit to see if you've skipped out on any previous landlords. He or she may also look for any court actions or other legal problems that might be red flags of a problem tenant. And, of course, landlords will look to see if you've ever been evicted from (kicked out of) a rental property in the past.

EMPLOYERS

More and more employers are doing credit checks on people they are considering hiring. This is especially common if the position involves money (for example, a bank teller). Some employers believe bad credit means that the individual is irresponsible and cannot be trusted to handle money. They may also believe an employee with a lot of debt may be more tempted to steal.

SCORE VS. REPORT: WHICH IS BETTER?

As we said, your credit report provides a thorough, detailed picture of your financial history, while your score is just, well, a three-digit number. If you have had credit issues, you are usually better off if the lender (or whoever is checking up on you) looks at the whole report. This way, the person checking can see if you just ran into a short-term problem that may have brought down your score. (Employers, for example, don't see your score; they see your report. So, if you can explain any minor or temporary issues you may have had in the past, you may be able to do damage control.)

WHAT TO DO IF YOUR REPORT ISN'T PERFECT

So you've had a few missteps, and there a couple of things on your credit report that aren't so great. What should you do? First, see if you can work with the creditor. Sometimes, the company will agree to remove the listing from your report if you pay what you owe.

If not, you are allowed to add a personal statement to your credit report. (You would contact the credit bureau to do this.) You should take this opportunity to explain any special circumstances that might show people this was an unusual event. For example, if you lost your job or had medical problems, you would want to include that information in your personal statement.

EXPERT ADVICE!
"My main tip for any young people is to pay their bills on time, particularly utility and cell phone bills. When we come out of high school, we generally have little to no credit rating. If people fail to pay a bill and allow it to become delinquent, such as a utility bill going unpaid for 90 days or more, it can become a collection on their credit report and drive down their good score or bury a minimal score!
A collection is an unpaid debt that will remain on a young person's credit report for seven years. Remember, you can be late on a utility bill for 89 days and no one needs to know about it. These are not like Visa card bills, which are late after 30 days. If you are late, no one needs to know about it beyond you and the utility company. But if you are late more than 89 days, your credit score will suffer for seven years."

~ Gregory B. Meyer, Community Relations Manager, Meriwest Credit Union

IF THERE ARE ERRORS IN YOUR REPORT

It is fairly common for credit reports to contain errors. A lender or creditor may have mistakenly reported your account as late, or your information may have gotten mixed up with someone else's. (This sometimes happens if you have a common name.)

Of course, there is also the possibility that the incorrect information is the result of fraud or identity theft. If you see a listing for an account you've never had or a lender you've never heard of, try contacting the company to see what information it can provide.

If you do spot errors or potentially fraudulent information, you should file a dispute with the credit bureau(s) right away. You can do this right on their Web site. The credit bureau will contact the person or business that provided the information and ask for verification or proof of the situation.

If you have been the victim of identity theft or fraud (or suspect you have been), you can add an alert to that fact on your credit reports. This will let people know that the information may be a result of fraudulent activity, not your own actions.

You can also add an alert that will require lenders to prove your identity before opening an account or granting a loan in your name. This prevents someone else from getting credit by posing as you.

DECIDING WHAT TO PAY FIRST

Okay, so let's say you run into a little bit of a financial dry spell, and you are having trouble paying all of your bills. What should you do? First, try calling you credit card companies or other service providers to see if they can offer you any options. Sometimes, they can change your payment due date or work out a payment plan to help you get back on track. Depending on the type of account, they may even be able to defer a payment or two.

After you do that, if you still don't have enough money to cover all of your payments, you will need to decide which bills get top priority. Any secured debt should be at the top of the list. Again, this is a loan that's secured by property, such as a house or car. If you are late on this type of loan, the lender can repossess your car or start to foreclose on your house.

Next, you should pay credit card bills. These are most likely to report late payments to credit agencies, which can hurt your credit. Utility companies are least likely to report late payments, so you usually have some wiggle room with them. However, keep in mind that they may suspend your service if your bill is past due, so you should always contact them to try to set up a payment arrangement to avoid that.

BUILDING GOOD CREDIT

You don't suddenly get good credit overnight. It can take time to establish good credit. (Remember, a portion of your credit score is based on the length of time you've had credit accounts.) And even once you've established credit, you need to work to keep it in good standing. If you've had a pitfall or two, you will need to work especially hard to get your credit back in shape and counteract the negative information.

The "secret" to building good credit boils down to this: Get credit, use it responsibly, and pay your bills on time. Of course, that's easier said than done.

HERE ARE SOME COMMON PITFALLS TO AVOID:

- **Going overboard on credit cards.** Be careful about opening too many credit cards, especially if you don't have a lot of experience handling credit. It's very tempting to want to use all those cards once you have them. A few shopping sprees later, your cards are all at their limit, and you have no idea how you will pay your bills.

• **Slacking off on the payments.** Even just one or two late or missed payments can really hurt your credit score. Do everything you can to make the payments on time, even if you can only pay the minimum.

• **Paying just the minimum.** If at all possible, you want to pay more than the minimum. Otherwise, it will take you a long time to pay off your balance, and you will end up paying a lot in interest fees.

• **Closing old accounts.** This is a common mistake. Many people think they should close old accounts they no longer use. In reality, this can hurt your credit score. (Remember, your score takes into account how long you've had credit, so keeping accounts you've had a long time can be a good thing.) To keep the account from seeming dormant, you should use it occasionally for a small purchase and then pay it off quickly.

CHAPTER 9
CHARGE IT!
(PAYING WITH PLASTIC)

Having a credit card can help you learn to handle credit responsibly and can also help you establish a credit history. And of course a credit card can come in handy if you have an emergency when you're short on cash. However, it's very easy to get into trouble by buying stuff you don't need and racking up big credit card bills you can't afford to pay. So owning a credit card really requires self-discipline and the ability to resist temptation when you see something you want to buy. (Even many adults have trouble keeping their plastic habit under control!)

CAN YOU GET A CARD?

It's not as easy for a younger person to get a credit card as it used to be. That's a good thing! Credit card companies are notorious for swarming college campuses and bombarding kids with offers for credit cards, even when students had no job and no way to pay the bill. A law passed in 2010 prevents anyone under 21 from getting a credit card unless he or she can prove there is enough income to pay the bill or get a co-signer. Still, more college students are incurring credit card debt each year. In fact, according to Sallie Mae, a government-funded lending institution, 76 percent of undergraduates have credit cards, and the average undergrad has $2,200 in credit card debt.

CREDIT CARD PROS AND CONS

As with anything, there are advantages and disadvantages to using credit cards. Before you acquire a piece of the plastic, think about the following pros and cons of credit card use.

ADVANTAGES

- **Immediate Access:** Need a new set of tires, but don't have $400? Credit can help. The best feature of credit cards is they can help you purchase expensive, unexpected emergency items and give you the flexibility to pay it over time.

- **Security:** If you lose your cash, it's gone, gone, gone. However, if you lose a credit card, it can be replaced. If you report a lost or stolen card promptly, you're protected against its unauthorized use.

- **Recordkeeping:** Your credit card statement is an itemized list of your monthly expenditures. This can be really helpful when you're working on your budget.

- **Convenience:** Credit cards are accepted at more places than checks, and they're generally faster to use.

- **Bill Consolidation:** You can pay your bills automatically via a credit card, consolidating several payments into a single lump sum.

- **Rewards:** Using a credit card with a rewards program may earn you benefits like free travel.

DISADVANTAGES

- **Interest and late fees:** Banks offer you credit, but they charge a steep price for the privilege of spending money you do not actually have. Credit card interest rates can range between 0 percent (this is most often just an introductory interest for a set amount of time) to as much as 22%, depending upon your credit score. For example, if you use your credit card to pay for that $30 pair of jeans, and you fail to pay off your monthly credit card bill, then that pair of jeans may actually cost $36.60. Remember that magic formula known as compound interest? This is one time where that factor works against you.

- **Easy to lose track of spending:** Paying with plastic is convenient but that could be a problem if you don't keep track of your spending. If you don't have a budget, and you don't stick to a set spending plan, paying with a credit card could allow you to rack up large amounts of debt without you even realizing it. Pay careful attention to your credit spending. Think of it as the same as cash, and pay off your credit card bill each month.

- **Increased chance of identity theft:** Each time you swipe your credit card, someone has access to two important items—your signature and your birth date. This makes it easier for people to steal your identity.

You can read more about using credit cards wisely at http://www.practicalmoneyskills.com/.

CREDIT CARD TERMS

Here are some helpful terms when it comes to credit cards:

- **Annual fee:** This is the fee a credit card company will charge you just for having the card, whether you use it or not. Not all cards have an annual fee—and for those that do, the fee can vary widely.

- **Annual percentage rate (APR):** This is the yearly interest rate you will be charged for any balance you carry on the card.

- **Balance:** This is the amount you owe on the card.

- **Grace period:** This is a period of time during which you can pay your balance without any interest charges.

- **Introductory rate:** Card companies will often lure you in by offering a low rate for an initial period when you first get the card. The problem: People often forget when this period will end, and then they suddenly find themselves paying a much higher rate as well as paying this rate retroactively.

- **Minimum payment:** This is the lowest amount you can pay on your monthly bill for a credit card account to keep the account in good status. If you only pay the minimum every month, you will end up paying a lot of interest charges.

> "College students have too many credit cards! Fifty percent of college students have four credit cards or more (per Sallie Mae). As a college student, I propose that all students carry just one credit card."
>
> ~ *Scott Gamm, 19-year-old student at NYU's Stern School of Business and founder of the personal finance Web site helpsavemydollars.com*

INTEREST WILL SNEAK UP ON YOU

When you buy things on credit, you pay interest, which keeps building over time if you don't pay off the full amount. If you're not careful, you could end up paying for that new computer or car stereo for years, and it could cost you hundreds of dollars more than you thought. Consider these basic purchases charged at the average 18% interest, with only minimum payments made every month:

Purchase	Interest Paid	Total Cost	Years to Pay off	Minimum Pmt
Phone ($300)	$ 59.45	$ 359.45	2 years	$15 per month
Laptop ($1,500)	$785.41	$2,285.41	5 years	$38 per month
Ski trip ($850)	$348.50	$1,198.50	4 years	$25 per month

–Source: Dollar Sensei, http://www.dollarsensei.com/TSAC/creditcards.htm

> Let's say you like to shop at H&M. You are out with friends at H&M and see a sweater you really like. Would you be happy if the clerk wanted to charge more than what's listed on the price tag? More than likely, you would not. That's what will end up happening when using a credit card and not paying off the balance—you will owe more for that clothing item because of interest. That's why it's important to pay off your credit card debt to avoid accruing interest and paying more.
> » Ornella Grosz, Author of *Moneylicious: A Financial Clue for Generation Y*

REMEMBER YOUR CREDIT LIMIT

Your credit card limit is the most you're allowed to spend, not how much you should spend. When you reach the limit, you'll be denied further charges, and it gets even harder to pay down. It also counts against your credit report when your balance is maxed out.

UNCOVER THE HIDDEN CHARGES

The fine print on credit card applications can get pretty interesting. Often, what looks like a great deal brings with it lots of hidden costs and what the banks refer to as "transaction fees." Here are some common extra charges that build up quickly:

- **Late fees:** Make a late payment, and you'll pay a late fee, which is sometimes equal to the minimum monthly payment.

- **Annual fees:** This is a yearly charge just for having the credit card, generally around $25–$50.

- **Over-limit fees:** This is a penalty charged for being over your credit limit.

INCREASED INTEREST

When you make multiple late payments—sometimes as few as two or three—the lender may increase your interest rate substantially.

Don't Take Cash Advances

Getting cash from your credit card when things are tight may seem like a great deal, but usually those cash advances come with strings attached. It's another way for the company to charge you a transaction fee, and usually you pay a higher interest rate on the advance than you do on regular purchases.

Stop New Offers by Opting Out

Remove your name from credit card mailing lists and opt out of new credit card offers by calling 888-5-OPT-OUT (888-567-8688) or visiting www.optoutprescreen.com. It's free and easy.

Do's and Don'ts of Credit Cards

- Do use it responsibly. It's not a free pass to buy anything you want.
- Don't forget your payment due date. The credit card company can tack on a hefty late charge even if you're only one day late.
- Do shop around to find the card with the best terms and/or perks.
- Don't go over your limit or you will get hit with an extra fee.
- Do contact the card company immediately if your card is ever lost or stolen.

CHOOSING A CREDIT CARD

There are a ton of credit cards out there. You may already be getting bombarded by offers in the mail and online. Don't make the mistake of thinking all credit cards are alike. There can be big differences, so you really need to shop around before you pick one.

EXPERT ADVICE!
Pay off all credit cards in full every month (highest rate first). A $5,000 credit card bill paid off at $100 a month will take nine years and $5,100 in additional interest charges. If you're paying 20% interest on credit card debt, action item number one is to pay it off before you do anything else. There's no point investing your money at a 10–15% gain, when it could be used to avoid a 20% loss.
~ Aaron Forth, VP and GM of Intuit Personal Finance Group

- Consider your habits and credit personality. Are you the type to pay off bills immediately? Do you have a lot of self-control when it comes to shopping, or do you tend to make a lot of impulse purchases? If you don't plan to carry a balance (you can pay off any charges within the grace period), then the interest rate may not matter so much to you. However, if you'll be carrying a balance, you will want to pay attention to the interest rate as those charges will add up quickly.

- Look at the interest rate. Even if you don't plan to make a lot of purchases or carry a balance, it's still good to try to find the best interest rate you can, just in case. Check out rewards. Many cards offer rewards points or other bonuses. Often, you can earn these points for doing things you would do anyway, such as buying snacks, if you pay for them with your credit card. The important thing here is to pay for your charges right away. Otherwise, any rewards you may earn will be outweighed by the interest charges you'll end up paying.

- Research any other fees. In addition to the interest rate, you may also end up paying other charges. The most common is the annual fee. Make sure to read the fine print in any credit card application to find out about these hidden fees.

There's no need to memorize your credit card number, but plenty of folks do know their credit card numbers by heart. Chances are they probably do a lot of online shopping! But what do the numbers on a credit card mean? Believe it or not, those numbers are not random. The 16 digits are there for a reason, and once you know what the different numbers mean, you can determine an awful lot about the credit card. You can learn to be a credit card sleuth.

Check out this info-graphic at TheMint.com to learn more about how to crack the credit card code: http://www.mint.com/blog/trends/credit-card-code-01202011/.

SECURED CREDIT CARDS

If you are just starting out and need to build credit (or have some credit issues and want to rebuild your credit), a secured credit card may be an option. This is a credit card, which is "secured" by a deposit you make into a connected account. Your credit limit is usually equal to the amount of your deposit. These are usually low-limit cards and may have a higher-than-average interest rate. But it can be a way for you to build credit, and often, once you use the card for a certain period of time, it switches to a regular credit card.

PREPAID CARDS

A prepaid card is just what it sounds like. You buy the card by paying an amount upfront, and then you have credit in that amount (minus any fees) available on that card. You can buy prepaid cards with a Visa or MasterCard logo at supermarkets and major retail chain stores. When you buy the card, you usually get a temporary card right there. You can only use this card in limited places and may run into challenges because it doesn't have your name on it. Usually, you can pay a few dollars to have a permanent card (with your name on it) sent to you by mail.

Prepaid cards eliminate the possibility of getting buried in debt or going overboard on your shopping. They also are less risky than using your bank cards—if the card is lost or stolen, someone cannot access your bank accounts with it or rack up a ton of charges in your name. The downside is that prepaid cards do not help you establish or build credit at all.

STUDENT PREPAID DEBIT CARDS

PayPal™ (the service that allows people to send money electronically) recently started a student debit card program. Parents set up the debit account, and the student gets a MasterCard® debit card with his or her own name on it that can be used online or in stores. Anyone 13 or older can get a card. It's a prepaid card, so the user can only spend the amount that's in the account. If the balance is too low, the card just won't work. However, a cool thing is that parents can transfer money into the account instantly—online or via their cell phone—which can come in handy in case of an emergency. Parents can also set up recurring payments, for example, if they want to give their student a certain allowance every week. For more information, check out https://student.paypal.com/ (click on the "student account" link in the bottom right corner).

Other student debit cards include the PASS card from American Express® and the Student UPside Visa® Prepaid Card, but be sure to check to see if there are monthly or annual fees.

Recent laws, including the Credit Card Accountability Responsibility and Disclosure Act (CARD Act), have forced credit card companies to be more transparent and have made it easier for people to deal with credit cards. Some changes include:

SAFEGUARDS AGAINST RATE INCREASES

- Under the Credit CARD Act, rate increases are prohibited during the first year and promotional rates must last for six months or longer.

- The Act prohibits "double cycle billing," where credit card holders are charged interest on debt that is paid on time during a grace period, and "universal default," where a lender changes a loan from the normal to the default terms when the consumer defaults with another lender.

- After the first year, cardholders must be notified of significant changes to the terms of an account 45 days before the changes take effect. New rates may not go into effect for 14 days after the notice of change is mailed. The consumer will also be afforded the option to cancel the account and pay off the balance at the existing rate.

IMPROVED BILLING PRACTICES

- The Credit CARD Act allows consumers 21 days to pay their monthly credit card bills (compared to the former minimum of 14 days).

- Payment due dates must fall on the same day of each month.

- Consumers must be allowed three weeks between the time a bill is mailed and the time it's due.

- Under the Act, credit card statements must appear in a specific font size for easier readability.

FEE RESTRICTIONS

- In almost all cases, consumers can't be charged for the method they use to pay their credit card bill (by check card, phone, mail, etc.).

- The Credit CARD Act limits fees consumers can be charged for spending over their credit limits.

- There are new limits to the fees consumers can be charged on subprime cards.

INCREASED DISCLOSURES

- Consumers must be provided with disclosures about how long it will take them to pay off a balance if only minimum payments are made.

- Credit card agreements must be available to consumers online.

- Under the Credit CARD Act, billing statements must include the payment due date, the minimum amount due, the ending balance, and detailed information about late fees.

PROTECTIONS FOR CONSUMERS UNDER 21

• Under the Act, consumers under 21 will only be able to get a credit card with proof of their ability to make payments independently or the help of an adult co-signer.

• The Act restricts incentives given to students who sign up for credit cards.

You can read more about this at http://www.practicalmoneyskills.com/.

QUIZ: WHAT'S YOUR CREDIT CARD I.Q.?

Answer **TRUE** or **FALSE:**

1. Credit cards are accepted as cash by stores.

2. Most credit cards have a credit limit.

3. If I pay my credit card in full by the due date, I will not owe any interest.

4. There's no penalty if I pay my balance after the due date.

5. If I pay the minimum monthly payment, then I won't owe any interest.

6. Credit card companies charge merchants a percentage of the price of anything purchased with a credit card.

7. My credit report contains information on bills I have not paid.

Answers:

1. TRUE. Actually, credit cards are a type of loan. You borrow money from the bank. The bank pays the store.

2. TRUE. Card holders may charge only up to a certain dollar amount set by the card company. The limit is set based on your ability to handle debt.

3. TRUE. If you pay the entire balance within the grace period allowed (usually about 28 days), you will not owe any interest on your purchases.

4. FALSE. Credit card companies charge late fees to card holders who do not pay their bill by the due date. Not paying your bill on time can be costly. Most credit card companies charge $25 or more to credit card users who fail to meet their deadlines—regardless of whether you pay the minimum due or the whole balance. In fact, you could pay a $35 penalty fee on a $15 balance.

5. FALSE. After you subtract the minimum payment from your balance, finance charges will be added to your remaining balance. So avoid the minimum payment trap. Pay your bill in full, or as close to in full as you can. The minimum payment is the least amount of money you can pay if you want to keep using your credit card. If you pay less than the minimum payment, the credit card company will often "turn off" your card so that it cannot be used to buy anything more. The card will not work again until you have made your minimum payment.

6. TRUE. When you use a credit card to make a purchase, the credit card companies charge the merchants a percentage of the sale.

7. **TRUE.** Actually, your credit report contains a lot more than that. It contains some vital non-credit facts, such as your name, nicknames, maiden name, marital status, spouse's name, social security number, year of birth, current and previous addresses, current and previous employers, and estimated income. Plus, it contains detailed information for each credit account you hold, including the type of account, when it was opened, the credit limit or loan amount, the balance you still owe, and whether you have been late with any payments. It also includes information such as lawsuits, bankruptcies, and liens against your property.

FINAL WORDS OF WISDOM

Be wise with your credit. Make sure you understand exactly how not to use a credit card, including avoiding only paying the minimum payments, which is a very common practice. Also, treat your credit card as though it were cash, and don't dig yourself into debt. The last thing you want is to graduate with thousands of dollars in credit card debt to add to your student loans.

At the same time, as long as you can remain disciplined, don't avoid a credit card altogether. Many avoid it thinking that it's the safest and smartest way to go, especially if they already have a debit card or cash. But in reality, the best way to build credit history and improve your credit score rating in college is to get a credit card, use it, and pay it off in full every month. Then, upon graduation, you will be at the top of creditors' lists when compared to your fellow graduates.

Don't underestimate the power of passive or side income. Not only can it help you get through college without financial stresses, but it can easily turn into a full-time business. For example, consider some of the top side business ideas out there in which you might be particularly passionate about. Running these businesses on the side can create some great income, develop your working skills while still in college, and set you up for an awesome career.

PART 6
MONEY U: PAYING FOR YOUR COLLEGE YEARS

College brings lots of new experiences and challenges—and plenty of new financial issues to consider. Tuition, books, groceries, nights on the town—it can all add up! We'll tell you how to apply for financial aid and scholarships to help pay for college, and we'll also share tips on managing your new assortment of expenses.

CHAPTER 10
FINANCIAL AID AND SCHOLARSHIPS

Unless you want to pay off college loans well into your 80s, financial aid will play a major role in your collegiate life. Financial aid is the amount of money you get from private and public sources for college. Usually the aid does not have to be paid back. With college costs higher than ever and the amount of college loan debt surpassing credit card debt for the first time, such aid is essential in determining your ability to go to the college of your choice and, for some students, whether they attend college at all. Aid from public and private sources—some based on various factors including race, academics, athletics, even whether you're left-handed—takes the pressure off your parents and your future earnings. But there's a lot of paperwork and red tape involved in applying for financial aid, and there are also some deadlines that are non-negotiable. So, you need to learn as much as you can about the financial process and the options available to you.

TYPES OF FINANCIAL AID

There are various types of financial aid. A student can earn scholarships, grants, federal help, and various aid awards for everything from academic achievement to being Catholic to even wearing a prom dress made out of duct-tape! When applying for college, it's important to learn about the various types of financial aid that are available so that you don't miss out on any opportunity. Below is a description of the different financial aid categories but to get a comprehensive list of all financial aid types available, check out *Peterson's Scholarships, Grants & Prizes 2013*.

Your Expected Family Contribution (EFC) plays a very important role in the financial aid process. The EFC is the government's way of determining how your family can pay for your college expenses. The higher the EFC, the less chance you have of financial aid. Your EFC is determined by the information you and your parents provide when you submit your application for the Free Application for Federal Student Aid (FAFSA).

GRANTS

A grant is a type of financial aid that generally is given to a student who demonstrates financial need. Grants do not need to be paid back.

PELL GRANT

The Pell Grant is the main federal grant program available to students with financial need. If you are eligible, several factors determine the amount of the grant you will actually get, including your EFC and whether you are in school full-time or part-time.

FSEOG

The Federal Supplemental Educational Opportunity Grant (FSEOG) is a grant reserved for the students most in need as determined by the school.

SCHOLARSHIPS

Scholarships can be awarded based either on financial need or merit (including your academic or athletic qualifications). Scholarship money doesn't need to be paid back—however, there may be some conditions you need to follow in order to keep your scholarship (for example, you may be required to keep your GPA at or above a certain level).

Use the following tips to help make your scholarship hunt successful.

- **Apply for scholarships early.** Your freshman year in high school is not too early to plan for scholarships by choosing extracurricular activities that will highlight your strengths and getting involved in your church and community—all things that are important to those who make scholarship decisions. Start your search by contacting your high school guidance counselor, who can give you the ins and outs on creating your scholarship plan of action.

- **Search for scholarships.** Be sure to check out *Peterson's Scholarships, Grants & Prizes*, an annual list of available private financial aid resources. Also, the easiest way to search for scholarships is through the Internet at Web sites such as www.finaid.org and http://studentaid.ed.gov. Scholarship information is also available at your local library.

- **Apply, apply, apply.** One student applied for nearly sixty scholarships and was fortunate enough to win seven. "Imagine if I'd applied for five and only gotten one," she says.

- **Plan ahead.** It takes time to get transcripts and letters of recommendation. Letters from people who know you well are more effective than letters from prestigious names who you know.

- **Be organized.** In the homes of scholarship winners, you can often find a file box where all relevant information is stored. This method allows you to review deadlines and requirements every so often. Computerizing the information, if possible, allows you to change and update information quickly. To learn the secrets to organizing your scholarship filing methods, check out *The "C" Student's Guide to Scholarships*, written by Felecia Hatcher, who received more than $100,000 in scholarship money despite having a GPA under 3.0.

- **Follow directions.** Make sure that you don't disqualify yourself by filling out forms incorrectly, missing a deadline, or failing to supply important information. Type your applications, if possible, and have someone proofread them.

FINDING AND GETTING ATHLETIC SCHOLARSHIPS

Are you an athlete? The following steps can help you attain an athletic scholarship:

1. **Contact the school formally.** Once you make a list of schools in which you are interested, get the names of the head coaches and write letters to the top twenty schools on your list. Then compile a factual resume of your athletic and academic accomplishments. Put together 10 to 15 minutes of video highlights of your athletic performance (with your jersey number noted), get letters of recommendation from your high school coach and your off-season coach, and include a season schedule.

2. **Ace the interview.** When you meet a recruiter or coach, be certain to exhibit self-confidence with a firm handshake and by maintaining eye contact. In addition, make sure that you are well groomed. According to recruiters, the most effective attitude is quiet confidence, respect, sincerity, and enthusiasm.

3. **Ask good questions.** Don't be afraid to probe the recruiter by getting answers to the following questions: Do I qualify athletically and academically? What are the parameters of the scholarship? For what position am I being considered? It's okay to ask the recruiter to declare what level of interest he or she has in you.

4. **Follow up.** Persistence pays off when it comes to seeking an athletic scholarship, and timing can be everything. A follow-up letter from your coach or a personal letter from you is extremely effective when it is sent: prior to your senior season, during or just after the senior season, just prior to or after announced conference-affiliated signing dates or national association signing dates, and mid- to late summer, in case other scholarship offers have been withdrawn or declined.

MYTHS ABOUT SCHOLARSHIPS AND FINANCIAL AID

The scholarship and financial aid game is highly misunderstood by many high school students. In addition, some high school guidance counselors often lack the time to fully investigate scholarship opportunities and inform students about them. (But you should still start your scholarship hunt at your counselor's office!) Myths and misconceptions persist while the truth about scholarships remains hidden, the glittering prizes and benefits unknown to many teenagers.

Myth 1: Scholarships are rare, elusive awards won only by valedictorians, geniuses, and brainiacs.

The truth is that with proper advice and strategies, private scholarships are within the grasp of high school students who possess talent and ability in almost any given field. Thousands of high school students like you compete and win. Even if you are only a "C" student, you can achieve scholarship success if you employ a bit of ingenuity and creativity. The era of the "academic" scholarships has expanded to include the "essay" scholarship, the "technology" scholarship, and even the "duct tape," scholarship where thousands of dollars are given to the prom couple who engineer, design, and create the most innovative prom attire using Duck Brand duct tape. The point is, even if you don't have academic prowess you can earn thousands of dollars in scholarship money to go to college if you're smart enough to look!

Myth 2: My chances of being admitted to a college are reduced if I apply for financial aid.

The truth is that most colleges have a policy of "need-blind" admission, which means that a student's financial need is not taken into account in the admission decision. A few colleges, however, do consider ability to pay before deciding whether to admit a student. A few more look at ability to pay of those whom they placed on a waiting list to get in or those students who applied late. Some colleges will mention this in their literature, but others may not. In making decisions about the college application and financing process, however, families should apply for financial aid if the student needs the aid to attend college.

Myth 3: All merit scholarships are based on a student's academic record.

The truth is that many of the best opportunities are in areas such as writing, public speaking, leadership, science, community service, music and the arts, foreign languages, and vocational-technical skills. So that means you don't always have to have a 3.99 GPA to win if you excel in a certain area.

Myth 4: You have to be a member of a minority group to get a scholarship.

The truth is that some scholarships are targeted toward women and minority students. Other scholarships require membership in a specific national club or student organization (such as 4-H or the National Honor Society), which makes these scholarships just as exclusive. Most scholarship opportunities, however, are not exclusive to any one segment of the population.

Myth 5: If you have need for and receive financial aid, it's useless to win a scholarship from some outside organization because the college will just take away the aid that the organization offered.

It's true that if you receive need-based aid, you can't receive more than the total cost of attendance (including room and board, books, and other expenses, not just tuition). If the financial aid that you've been awarded meets the total cost and you win an outside scholarship, colleges have to reduce something. But usually they reduce the loan or work-study portion of your financial aid award before touching the grant portion that they've awarded you. This means that you won't have to borrow or earn as much at a job. Also, most colleges don't meet your full financial need when you qualify for need-based financial aid. So, if you do win an outside scholarship, chances are that your other aid will not be taken away or reduced.

LOANS

Though student loans are collectively known as financial aid, they are really just deferred aid. You must pay them back. For most students, the majority of their financial aid comes in the form of student loans. These loans are backed by the federal government, have decent interest rates, and don't require a credit check. However, they can add up quickly, and you will usually have to start paying them back soon after you finish school.

Since July 1, 2010, all federal education loans are now made through the Direct Loan program. The loans are made through the college's financial aid office, with funds provided by the U.S. Department of Education. This includes the Federal Parent PLUS loan in addition to student loans.

DIRECT STAFFORD LOAN

Stafford loans come in two types: subsidized and unsubsidized. The type you qualify for will depend on your level of financial need. With unsubsidized loans, the interest accrues while you are in school, which can add quite a bit to the balance you owe. The repayment term is ten years, although that can be extended if the student uses the income-based repayment option.

FEDERAL PERKINS LOAN

The Federal Perkins Loan is given by colleges to students who have the most financial need. This loan is subsidized, meaning interest does not accrue while you're in school.

A Warning about Borrowing Too Much for School

Education debt can have a big impact on your lifestyle after graduation. Students who graduate with no debt are almost twice as likely to go on to graduate from a professional school as students who graduate with some debt. Students who graduate with excessive debt or who default on their loans are more likely to be depressed. They often delay getting married, having children, buying a car, and buying a home. Borrowing excessively can be like having a mortgage without owning a home. The debt may make it more difficult to save for retirement or your own children's college educations.

– Courtesy of www.fastweb.com

PLUS LOANS

PLUS loans are available to parents or graduate students. Unlike other government student loans, PLUS loans do take the applicant's credit rating into account. (However, if your parent is denied a PLUS loan due to bad credit, you are then allowed to borrow an additional amount in student loans. The PLUS loan has an interest rate of 7.9 percent, along with 4 percent fees.

PRIVATE STUDENT LOANS

Private loans (sometimes called alternative loans) are given by banks and other financial institutions. They often require a credit check. The terms of these loans can vary from lender to lender.

According to FinAid.org, two thirds (65.6 percent) of four-year undergraduate students graduated with a bachelor's degree had some debt in 2007–08, and the average student loan debt among graduating seniors was $23,186 (excluding PLUS Loans but including Stafford, Perkins, state, college, and private loans). Among graduating four-year undergraduate students who applied for federal student aid, 86.3 percent borrowed to pay for their education, and the average cumulative debt was $24,651.

APPLYING FOR FINANCIAL AID

You want to make sure you look into the financial aid process way ahead of time because there are deadlines you must meet, and if you are too late, you'll be out of luck.

Here are the main things you need to do (although your situation may vary, so be sure to check with your school's financial aid office, just to make sure you don't overlook anything).

- **Complete the FAFSA.** This is the Free Application for Federal Student Aid and is required for any federal aid. You can complete the FAFSA online at www.fafsa.ed.gov. You can submit the FAFSA on or after January 1, so many people do it right after New Year's so as not to forget.

- **Complete your state financial aid application (if needed).** Some states don't have their own financial aid form—they just go by the information you submitted on the FAFSA. Check with your state's department of education to find out for sure.

- **Complete the CSS/Financial Aid PROFILE.** Some schools (mainly private schools) also require another form called the CSS/Financial Aid PROFILE. This is a pretty detailed form and can take a while to complete, so be sure to ask as soon as possible if your school uses it, so you leave enough time to finish it.

ONLINE FINANCIAL AID RESOURCES

> ### Need a little extra help?
> Staff members at your school's financial aid office are always available to help you find ways to manage your money. Don't hesitate to ask for their help; simply make an appointment to get yourself on a clear path to financial success.

You can get a ton of information about financial aid—and can even complete and submit most financial aid applications—online. If you have specific colleges in mind, be sure to check out the financial aid section on their Web site. You especially want to pay attention to any of these deadlines since these may be different than the deadlines for state or federal financial aid—and you want to make sure you aren't late.

Here are some sites you should check out:

FAFSA ONLINE

The Free Application for Federal Student Aid (FAFSA) is the form you must complete in order to receive any federal financial aid, including student loans. Even if you don't think you will qualify for aid (say, because your parents make too much money), you should still complete the FAFSA. It's free, and you might be surprised to find that you do qualify for aid. And besides, many schools require you to complete the FAFSA if you want to apply for any scholarships from the school. You can complete the FAFSA online at www.fafsa.ed.gov.

NELNET, INC.

Nelnet is one of the leading education planning and finance companies in the United States and is focused on providing quality college planning and financing products and services to students and schools nationwide. Nelnet offers a broad range of financial services and technology-based products, including student loan origination, loan consolidation guarantee servicing, and software solutions. Visit the Web site at www. nelnet.com.

FINAID

FinAid is a comprehensive source of information and advice related to financial aid. The site also has links to a bunch of scholarship search sites. Visit the FinAid site at http://www. finaid.org/.

Quick Tips from Nelnet:

You can save on interest and repay your loans sooner by making early payments or adding a little on to your regular payment whenever you're able.

If you choose a plan and it doesn't work, you can switch your plan up to once a year by contacting your lender or servicer.

Whenever you move, you should be sure to call your lender or servicer so that they have your new mailing address and contact numbers.

It's important to keep track of your loans—everything from the loan amount to the repayment start date. Using a chart like the following one may be just what you need to stay organized and on top of all of this important financial matter. Feeling creative? Make your own student loan chart—one that you'll be inclined to fill in and track!

Tracking Your Student Loans						
Academic Period	Loan Type	Lender/ Loan Holder	Servicer	Loan Amount	Interest Rate	Repayment Start Date

Record of Communication					
Date	Loan Type and Account No.	Organization	Contact Person	Phone No.	Reasons for communication

COMMON QUESTIONS ABOUT STUDENT LOAN REPAYMENT

What are my options?

The best way to repay will depend mostly on your individual circumstances. The choices include:

- **Standard:** You pay monthly installments of at least $50 over a ten-year period, with payments based on the amount you borrowed. This option is the most common and generally the most economical.

- **Extended:** If you have more than $30,000 in Stafford loans borrowed after October 7, 1998, you may be eligible to extend the term of your payments for up to twenty-five years. Remember, though, that a longer term adds interest to your overall balance.

- **Graduated:** If your loan balance is high or your income low, you may choose this plan because it offers lower payments to start, gradually increasing over time, with up to ten years to repay. However, the amount of interest you pay overall is higher than with standard repayment.

- **Income-sensitive:** Payments are determined by comparing your debt to your monthly income, are adjusted annually, and can only be used for five years. After that time, payments revert to the standard plan.

- **Income-based Repayment:** Available to borrowers who display partial financial hardship. Payments are based on your adjusted gross income, family size, and balance on eligible loans.

What happens if I pay late or default on my loan?

Think of paying back your student loans as your end of the deal—you're obligated to repay the debt just like any other. Paying on time offers huge rewards for your financial future, but late payments and defaulting on your debt have serious consequences, such as:

- A poor credit rating that will keep you from getting a car or home loan

- Losing the option to make monthly payments and end up owing your entire balance at once

- Piling up late charges and collection fees

- Garnished wages

What programs are out there to help get me back on track?

- **Deferment:** If your lender approves it, you may be able to temporarily stop making payments for reasons such as economic hardship, unemployment, or returning to school full-time. With deferment, interest on subsidized Stafford and Perkins loans is paid. For unsubsidized loans, though, you'll still be responsible for paying the interest.

- **Forbearance:** As with deferments, being granted forbearance means your payments are temporarily postponed. Your lender must approve the forbearance. During forbearance, you'll still be responsible for paying the interest that builds on your loans.

- **Consolidation:** If you have multiple loans through multiple lenders, you may find it more efficient and less expensive over the long term to consolidate all of your loans into one larger loan. You'll need to carefully weigh the circumstances, though, calculating things like whether your monthly payments are substantially lowered, how much (if any) additional interest you'll pay, and more.

CHAPTER 11
MANAGING YOUR FINANCES WHILE IN COLLEGE

College is a training ground for the real world. In college, you're forced to start acting like an adult doing "grown-up" things like paying your own bills, but you aren't totally on your own yet, so you still have some sort of safety net.

PRACTICE BEING INDEPENDENT

If you're like a lot of college students, your parents may still be helping you out financially while you're in school. Even if they no longer pay your bills or give you an allowance, they may be helping in ways that aren't as obvious. For example, you may still be covered under their health insurance policy, which makes your costs much cheaper than if you had to get coverage on your own.

It's easy to become a little lax when it comes to money and staying on top of your finances because you know your parents will be there to help you out if you get stuck. And while it's nice to have that safety net, this can also serve as a sort of crutch that prevents you from becoming totally independent and taking your own financial responsibility seriously.

Even before you enter college, you should check your credit report. Even if you've never had a loan, you probably still have something on your credit report. Don't think so? You might be surprised. A study conducted by Sallie Mae found that only 2 percent of undergraduates had no credit history.

177

So you may need to pretend your parents don't exist (financially speaking) for a month or so, just to see how well you do. (This will also help spotlight areas where you might need to brush up your skills or get more information.) Obviously, you can always ask your parents for help if you have an emergency or really run into trouble, but it's good to get into the habit of handling things on your own as much as possible. Think of it as a practice run at being a self-sufficient adult. You probably are capable of doing more than you think, and it can be a big confidence boost to know you don't need your parents to do everything for you anymore.

NO SUCH THING AS NORMAL

There really is no such thing as a "typical" college student these days. Many adults are going back to school to complete their degree or earn another one in order to help their career. Some people in their 20s may have had a delay in their path to college because they had to get a job or were serving in the military. A lot of students are opting to stay at home and commute to school in order to save money. And an increasing number of students are taking some or all of their classes online from home.

> # Fun Fact
> A study of student spending by Yale students in 1915 found that one freshman spent $4,500 in his first year. That's the equivalent of more than $94,000 today!

Your budget and financial issues will vary from those of your fellow students, depending on your individual circumstances. So don't waste too much energy comparing yourself to them. Yes, it's easy to get bummed out if one of your classmates seems to have an endless supply of money. But it's very possible that she took out a lot of student loans (which she is now spending recklessly) and will soon find herself with mega debt.

FOR THE DORM DWELLERS

If you live on campus, you may only have limited financial issues to deal with (as far as living expenses go—tuition and school expenses are a whole separate issue). Your basic living expenses are probably all bundled into your housing costs, and you are likely required to have a meal plan, which will take care of some of your food expenses.

But depending on what type of meal plan you have (and what you eat), you will probably need some extra money for snacks and additional meals off campus. And you will also have to pay for your cell phone and any other bills you have. If you have a roommate, the two of you may also decide to jointly buy some things for the room.

According to one survey, college students receive an average of $312 per month from home and have $453 in monthly earnings.

There is also the cost of transportation. You may need to pay for transportation to get around campus or to travel off campus for errands or to get to work. And of course you will need to pay for trips back home. The average college student living on campus spent $1,073 on transportation in 2010–11.

There are lots of other "little" expenses that can quickly add up. Think about your laundry, for example. You will probably be surprised at how much change those washers and dryers can eat up!

So even if you don't have an apartment, a car, or other major expenses, you will spend some money every month while at school, and you need to have a plan for how you will pay for that.

OFF-CAMPUS LIVING

If you are thinking about living off campus, you may be looking forward to having some "freedom" without your RA or other college authorities being able to tell you what to do. On the flip side, though, you will have additional expenses and other issues to consider, things you wouldn't need to worry about if you lived on campus.

First, you will need to find an apartment. Your school's housing office may be able to connect you with some leads or suggest resources for finding off-campus rentals.

TIP

Rents are often highest for apartments closest to campus, because landlords figure you'll pay more for this convenience. If you are willing to live further away from campus and walk or take the bus to school, you may be able to find more affordable housing.

Before you start looking, you must examine your budget and figure out what you can afford per month. Look around to see what's available and see how the average rents compare to your monthly figure. Be sure to factor in the cost of utilities, if they aren't included in the rent. If the rents are too high for you on your own, calculate the cost when it is split with another person (or several). Keep in mind that you may have to pay a security deposit upfront—usually one month's rent, but occasionally even more than that.

When you find an apartment you like, you will probably have to complete a rental application. This may ask about your income, because the landlord wants to be sure you'll be able to afford the rent every month. The landlord may also do a background check to see if you have good credit and make sure you haven't been evicted from an apartment in the past. (See Chapter 7 for more about credit checks.)

If you don't have a job or other source of income, or if the landlord is nervous about renting to you because of your age, you may get asked to get a co-signer. Your parents may

---

180

be willing to do this, but it's important that you remember that it is your responsibility to pay this bill. Don't leave your parents holding the bag.

> A **co-signer** is someone who signs a loan or rental application with you. This person agrees to be responsible for that debt, should you fail to pay it.

If you decide you want the apartment (and the landlord approves you as a tenant), you will need to sign a lease or rental agreement. This is a contract that states how much you will pay—monthly rent, security deposits, and any other charges you may be required to pay. It usually also spells out all of the rules you must follow, from how you must maintain the property to whether you are allowed to have overnight guests.

Be sure to read this document carefully. It's a good idea to have your parents look it over, too. Watch for any fine print, especially any charges or fees the landlord can impose (say, a late fee if your rent isn't on time or a "cleaning fee" if the landlords feels the place is messy when you move out).

The lease is a legal document, and you will be obligated to abide by its terms. It can be difficult to break a lease, and if you move out of the apartment before your lease is up, you will often be held responsible for any rent due for the remaining term of the lease.

ARE YOU READY FOR ROOMMATES?

Most likely, you won't be able to afford a place of your own, so you will probably need to live with roommates. In addition to all of the normal roommate issues you would encounter if you lived in the dorms (getting used to each other's bad habits, coordinating schedules so you can each study, sleep, or do other daily activities in peace, etc.), you will also have financial matters to sort out.

If you don't know your roommates well (or at all), you have no idea how they manage their money. They may be shopaholics who have trouble paying their bills, or they may be obsessive about splitting the bills equally right down to the penny.

It's important to iron out the financial details in advance of move-in day. Discuss them in as much detail as possible- to try to prevent problems later. Make a list of every expense— including things like groceries and cleaning supplies, if you will be sharing these items. Then discuss how you want to divide up the bills.

Think about how you want to handle things you may not use equally. For example, if there's a charge for a parking spot and only one of you has a car, this may not be a cost you need to split.

Try to go through every possible scenario you can think of, so you'll be prepared to handle any money situations that may crop up. Even if you'll be sharing a place with friends, that's no guarantee that you won't run into money issues and financial disagreements.

Ideally, your landlord or property management company allows for individual leases. That means you each enter into a separate rental agreement with the landlord and are only responsible for your own rent. That way, if your roommate flakes out or disappears, you aren't on the hook for his or her part of the rent.

ROOMMATE MONEY QUESTIONS TO CONSIDER

- What happens if one person drops out of school or otherwise needs to vacate early?

- If one roommate loses his job or can't pay the rent, what happens?

• Do you share groceries and household supplies? If not, how will you make sure one person doesn't use stuff the other person bought?

• What about guests? What if a guest damages something or uses some household supplies?

KEEP CREDIT CARDS UNDER CONTROL

Once they escape their parents' watchful eye, many college students become more reckless with their spending, especially if they want to buy cool clothes or enjoy lots of social activities with their friends. This is when it gets very tempting to rely on plastic to pay for all your splurges. It's important to be self-disciplined enough to resist racking up big credit card bills. To make things easier, avoid getting a lot of credit cards in the first place. You really only need one credit card, just for emergencies.

Credit card companies traditionally put a lot of effort into marketing to college students. They would host big promotions on campus and give away free swag to students who signed up. They would usually gladly give you a credit card even if you had no job and no apparent means of paying the bill.

> According to one study, the average college student has a credit card balance of $3,173. Around 21 percent of undergraduates have balances between $3,000 and $7,000.

Recent laws have had a major impact on how credit card companies can market—and provide credit cards—to students [see Chapter 9: Charge It! (Paying with Plastic)]. It's now tougher to get a credit card if you're under 21, and that's a good thing, as it helps protect you from getting buried in sky-high credit card bills.

BE SMART WITH STUDENT LOAN DEBT

If you're like many college students, you may have no choice but to take out some student loans in order to help pay for college. But if you get a tax refund because you have excess financial aid (and some of that consists of loans), it's a smart idea to contact the financial aid office and tell them you want to decrease the amount of your loans. Remember, this isn't "free money." Loans are a debt that you will need to repay, so you shouldn't take more than you absolutely need.

YOUR INCOME MAY AFFECT YOUR FINANCIAL AID

If you receive financial aid for school, keep in mind that your income may affect how much aid you can receive. (It can seem like an unfair Catch-22: You are trying to improve your financial situation by working, but then the government or your school may turn around and cut the amount of money they'll give you in aid.)

Check with your school's financial aid office for advice and information on how an increase in income may affect your aid. Some forms of income (such as pay from a work-study job) do not affect your aid. If your income will affect your aid, you need to weigh the different scenarios and see how you would come out better.

SAVE MONEY ON TEXTBOOKS

> The average costs for books and materials for a four-year public university in 2010–11 was $1,137.

Even if your tuition costs are covered by financial aid (or paid by your parents), you may still need to pay for your textbooks out of your own pocket. If you've never bought a textbook before, prepare for sticker shock. Even a relatively thin paperback book can be shockingly expensive.

EXPERT ADVICE!
"Save on textbooks: Don't purchase textbooks at the school bookstore. I saved $300 last year by buying used textbooks and renting textbooks. Use the free textbook search engine at helpsavemydollars.com to find the cheapest textbook retailers."
~ Scott Gamm, 19, student at NYU's Stern School of Business and founder of helpsavemydollars.com

You can usually save lots of money by buying used textbooks. Check out the bulletin boards on campus—or the local CraigsList or other online classifieds—to see if anyone is selling the books you need. Better yet, rent your books. You can use sites like Chegg.com to rent books online.

BEWARE THE UNPAID INTERNSHIP

Internships are popular with college students because you can gain work experience and possibly earn college credit while also making some extra money. But many companies are now offering internships that don't pay at all. In many cases, these companies are actually ignoring the law. The government has rules about internships, and there are only limited situations when it's okay for a company not to pay an intern. Most of the time, companies are required to pay interns, even though many of them try to get away without doing so.

The U.S. Department of Labor specifies the rules regarding unpaid internships on its Web site at www.dol.gov.

Some major companies offer unpaid internships—and, as one college intern ship counselor noted, it often follows that the more popular the company is with college students (think sports and media companies), the less likely they are to pay interns. That's because many college students are so eager to work for these companies, they are willing to do it for free just for the "prestige" of working there and adding it to their resume.

If you are tempted to take an internship that doesn't come with a paycheck, think carefully and weigh the pros and cons. The internship may actually end up costing you money, especially if you need to find housing in whatever city the internship is located.

TIP

The Jump$tart Coalition Reality Check interactive tool at http://jumpstart.org/reality-check-page1.html lets you enter some information about your lifestyle habits and future plans, and then it gives you an estimate of how much money you will need. This can definitely be a wake-up call!

MAINTAIN YOUR MONEY HABITS

Hopefully, at this point, you have already developed some money management skills and feel comfortable with the budgeting basics. (If not, it's not too late—just go back and review some of the earlier chapters in this book for tips.) But mastering your money isn't just a one-time thing. You need to keep up these good habits for life. Some tips for staying in the groove:

• Do a basic review of your budget every month, especially if your situation changes (say, you start a new job) or you have trouble making ends meet.

• Be diligent about checking your online bank activity regularly to keep track of your balances and watch for any signs of trouble. Make this a part of your daily routine (it only takes a few minutes).

• Review a copy of your credit report every few months, and look at it closely to check for mistakes or outdated information.

PART 7
TAKING STOCK OF YOUR FINANCIAL FUTURE: INVESTING

Investing is a great way to help plan for your future. It can also be really cool to watch your money grow, if you invest it wisely. You don't need to be a millionaire to invest—taking a little bit from each paycheck is a great way to start. Anything you can stash away now will help you create a nest egg for your future. We know the thought of investing can be intimidating, so we've broken it down into simple terms to make investing easier.

CHAPTER 12
INVESTING: HOW TO MAKE YOUR MONEY GROW

Financial investing is when you put money into something with the expectation that you will earn more than what you put in. People invest in all kinds of money-making vehicles from company stocks and financial accounts to commodities such as corn and rice and even in real estate and oil and gas. Remember that wonderful force called Compound Interest? Investing is when CI works for you! But while investing seems like a quick way to make a buck, it comes with substantial risk. Unlike putting money in a bank, where it's federally insured, there is little or no insurance against losing all the money you invest. The key to investing is simple: patience. If it's too good to be true it probably is, and though most people do not like to hear it, the best way to use money to make money is to invest for the long term. This chapter explains the different options offered for investing. Unlike many cool activities, there is not an age limit on investing. In fact, you've probably already investing—if you're parents have bought you a U.S Savings Bond or if you have a money market or a savings account. Those are low-risk investment vehicles.

THE GAME OF RISK

When you invest, there is no guarantee that you will make money, and, in some cases, you may lose all the money you invested! The risk varies depending on the type of investment. Some investments (like bonds) are said to be no-risk or low-risk. The downside is that you won't earn as much potential profit from these low-risk choices. In order to possibly earn really big profits, you need to take some risks. (Of course, most people who choose risky investments always think they've found a "sure thing" that will definitely pay off. The lure of a big payday is very tempting and can cause people to ignore the risk of losses.)

The chart below (courtesy of TheMint.org) shows the risk levels of the most common types of investments.

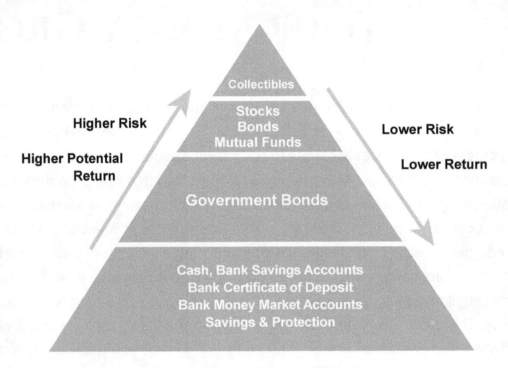

DOING THE DIVERSIFICATION DANCE

The perfect scenario when it comes to investing is having limited risk while also having the potential for some nice returns on your investment. One way to do this is by diversifying. This means you divide up your money and invest it in a bunch of different money-making vehicles that have varying degrees of risk. Some investments may be low-risk, while others would be higher risk (with the chance for bigger rewards). If you don't want to chance losing too much, you would put most of your money in low-risk investments.

LIQUIDITY

Another thing to consider with investments is how easy it will be to get your money when you want it. This is called liquidity. With some types of investments, your money is tied up for a specific period of time, and you won't be able to get access to it (or if you do, you may be charged a penalty fee).

STOCK MARKET

One of the most popular ways to invest is through the stock market. A stock is a piece of ownership in a company. (So, yes, you could technically say you are a part-owner of the company, but your piece of the company is usually small.) When you buy stock in a company, you are known as a shareholder. Not all companies have stock available. A company sells shares in order to raise money to expand, hire more employees, or for other reasons.

Want to have some fun while learning a lot about the stock market? TD Bank offers a "Fantasy Stock Market" game, where you can "virtually" play the stock market with $100,000 fantasy dollars. You can check stock quotes, look up ticker symbols, learn stock market terminology, track your daily performance, and compete against your friends. You can find this game on the TD Bank Web site at http://virtualstockmarket.tdbank.com/.

The stock market is where stocks are traded (bought and sold). The goal is to buy a stock at a cheap price, and then sell it once it is worth a lot more. This is known as buying low and selling high. Unfortunately, many people try to reach this goal within weeks. This is NOT the way to invest. Remember, stock investing is a marathon, not a sprint. If you try to get rich quick, you will increase your risk and the stock market will feel like a roller coaster.

Within a span of a week, your stock's value may go up and down, and up and down again. Stocks are not guaranteed by the government or anyone else. There is the possibility that you could lose most or all of your money. The why to invest in stocks is to forget about the money and let it rest for a long period of time. Watching the daily differences in your stock price can be hazardous to your health!

SOME IMPORTANT STOCK MARKET TERMS

Asset: Something that will rise in price and can be sold for more money.

Bear Market: The time when stock prices fall for a while. Many people believe this is a good time to buy stocks.

Blue Chip: A large company's stock that is likely to be low risk. Microsoft and Apple are good examples.

Bond: Sold to get money to start up a business or support the government. It collects interest over time.

Bull Market: The time when stock prices go up for a while. This is when people try to sell their stocks.

Capital: Money used to try to get more money. For example, the purchase price of your stock is your capital.

Inflation: When the price of everything goes up. In 1980, the cost of a regular gallon of gas was about $1.25. Compare that to what you pay when you fill up your car's tank today—that's inflation!

Portfolio: The collection of all of your investments.

Profit: The money you make after selling stock.

Stock: Partial ownership of a company. It's like sharing, but sometimes everybody loses everything.

CHECK OUT MY CDS

Certificates of deposit (called CDs) are investments in which you deposit a certain amount of money (usually at least several hundred dollars) for a specific period of time. The interest rate varies depending on the type of CD, but because there is virtually no risk, the interest rate isn't as high as other, riskier investments. Like bank accounts, CDs are insured by the government, so you cannot lose your money.

When you put your money into a CD, you agree to keep it there for a certain period of time. If you try to withdraw your money early, you will pay a penalty.

MONEY MARKET ACCOUNTS

A money market account is an investment account you open through a bank. The bank invests your money in low-risk places and pays you interest. The interest can vary from day to day. The bank may require you to invest a minimum amount in order to avoid fees. You can take your money out when you want. Here's a tip on making money while buying something you want. Often, stores will offer you a "same as cash" deal on a purchase. This means they issue a credit to purchase something without interest for a certain amount of time. Take this option, but don't make the monthly payment. Instead take the monthly payment and deposit it into a money market account for the same amount of time. When the time limit is up, pay off the credit purchase, and you'll have extra money in your pocket!

MUTUAL FUNDS

Mutual funds are sort of a combination of the stock market and diversification. You give your money to a broker or fund manager, who invests it (along with money from many other people) into a bunch of different places that may include stocks, bonds, real estate investments, and others. Usually, a mutual fund will combine a variety of low-risk and higher-risk investments. So, you still have some risk, but it is usually less than with the stock market. The interest rate you earn will depend on how well the investments do.

GOVERNMENT BONDS

U.S. government bonds are considered among the safest types of investments because they are guaranteed by the federal government. They became very popular several decades ago during major wars when the government sold bonds in order to raise money to pay for war costs. They are still popular because of the lack of risk. The downside is that your money is tied up for a certain period of time (usually quite a few years). The EE bonds allow you to double your money, but will take a long time. Say you want a $100 bond. You pay $50, and then you must wait for the bond to reach its maturity date, which will be years later. At that time, you can cash in the bond and get your hundred bucks.

REAL ESTATE

Some people like to invest in real estate. This isn't something everyone can do, though, because you need to have a lot of cash available in order to buy, maintain, and possibly fix up properties. People who invest in real estate will either keep the property and rent it out (becoming a landlord) or wait for its value to increase and then sell it for a profit.

COLLECTIBLES

Some people like to buy collectibles as an investment. Collectibles could include anything from baseball cards to sports cars. When you invest in items like these, you are counting on the fact that they will increase in value as time passes. But there is no guarantee that will happen, and there are lots of stories of people who bought a lot of things they thought would be collectible, only to later have to unload them cheap on eBay or at a garage sale.

GLOSSARY

Adjustable rate: an interest rate that can change depending on the economy or other circumstances.

Allowance: an amount of money that someone (usually a parent) provides on a regular basis as spending money.

Annual fee: fee a credit card company will charge you just for having the card, whether you use it or not. Not all cards have an annual fee—and for those that do, the fee can vary widely.

Annual percentage rate (APR): yearly interest rate you will be charged for any balance you carry on a credit card.

Asset: something that will rise in price and can be sold for more money.

ATM: automated teller machine, which you can use to make deposits and withdraw cash from your bank account.

Balance: amount of money in your bank account at a given time; amount owed on a credit card.

Barter: to trade one thing for another. If you have something another person wants, and they have something you want, you can make a trade that makes both of you happy.

Bear Market: a period when stock prices fall for a while.

Blue Chip: a large company's stock that is likely to be low risk.

Bond: sold to get money to start up a business or support the government. It collects some interest over time.

Borrow: to take out a loan. You obtain money from a person or business (usually a bank or loan agency) and agree to pay it back with interest.

Bounced check: a check that exceeds the balance of your bank account and causes your account to become overdrawn (go into the negative). Your bank may honor the check or return it unpaid, but, either way, you will probably be charged a fee.

Budget: a plan of how you will spend and/or save your money.

Bull Market: a period when stock prices go up for a while.

Capital: money used to start up a business or fund a project

Compound interest: when interest accumulates and is added to the principal, causing a sort of "snowball effect." You end up paying interest on previous interest charges that have been added to the principal.

Contract: a written agreement between two people or parties that spells out the terms for a loan, sale, or other business transaction.

Co-signer: someone who signs a loan or rental application with you. This person agrees to be responsible for that debt, should you fail to pay it.

Credit report: a history of what you've borrowed and how you have paid your debts.

Credit score: a 3-digit number that is calculated based on your credit report. Lenders and businesses use your credit score to decide whether to approve you for credit or a loan.

Debit Card: card linked to a bank account, usually a checking account, used to pay for things instead of cash or check. You can only spend as much as you have in your bank account at that time; otherwise, your transaction will probably be declined, or your account will become overdrawn.

Debt: money that you owe to someone. Debt is often the result of a loan or a credit account.

Deposit: money put into a bank account.

Direct deposit: when your paycheck or other payment is automatically deposited into your bank account.

EFC: Expected Family Contribution, a figure calculated by the government to help determine your financial need for student aid. The higher your EFC, the less chance you have of financial aid.

Entrepreneur: someone who starts his or her own business.

FDIC: Federal Deposit Insurance Corporation, a federal agency that insures your bank account, covering your deposits (up to $250,000).

FICA: Federal Insurance Contributions Act, which allows for deduction from your paycheck to fund Social Security and Medicare programs.

Finance charge: costs that a business (such as a bank or credit company) adds to your debt as a fee for providing or servicing the loan or account.

Fixed rate: an interest rate that stays at one amount for the length of the loan.

Grace period: period of time during which you can pay your balance without any interest charges.

Gross pay: amount you earn before deductions.

Income: money that you earn as pay for doing a job.

Installment loan: a type of credit in which you borrow a certain amount of money that is to be used for a specific purpose. You must make a monthly payment until the balance is paid off. Examples of installment loans are mortgages and car payments.

Interest: fee paid to use money. When you deposit money in an account, you earn interest. When you borrow money, you pay interest.

Introductory rate: a low interest rate a credit card company offers you for a short time when you first open an account.

Inflation: a rise in the prices for goods and services over time.

Line of credit: a pre-approved loan that you can get money from as you need it. You only borrow what you need (or want) and only pay interest on that amount.

Medicare: an insurance program run by the federal government that provides medical insurance to the elderly and disabled. The program is funded through taxes that are collected in the form of payroll deductions.

Minimum payment: the lowest amount you can pay on your monthly bill for a credit card account to keep the account in good status. If you only pay the minimum every month, you will end up paying a lot of interest charges.

Mortgage: loan from the bank used to buy a house.

Net pay: amount of your actual paycheck after all deductions. This can often be shocking, because the deductions can take a big chunk of your paycheck.

PIN number: Personal Identification Number, the security code used to access your account.

Portfolio: collection of all of your investments.

Prime rate: the very best interest rate, which is usually only available to borrowers with the best credit.

Principal: the amount of money you borrowed (or deposited into an account) before any interest charges are added.

Profit: money you make when you sell something, after deducting all of your expenses and costs.

Resume: a document that lists your work experience, education, references, and other important information that potential employers (or customers) would want to know. You use this when you are trying to get a job.

Revolving credit: also known as a revolving account, this is a type of credit account that you can keep using over and over (assuming you make your required payments and stay under your credit limit). Types of revolving accounts include credit cards and home equity lines of credit.

Secured credit card: a credit account for which you deposit a certain amount to guarantee the debt. You can only borrow an equivalent to your deposit amount, and if you don't pay your bill, your deposit is used to satisfy the debt.

Social Security: a federal government program that provides monetary benefits for the elderly, disabled, and (in some cases) survivors of individuals who have died. These payments are funded by money collected in the form of deductions from paychecks.

Stock: partial ownership of a company.

Stock market: the system for buying and selling shares for a bunch of different companies.

Withdrawal: money taken out of an account.

RESOURCES

BOOKS

Kofke, Danny. 2011. *A Simple Book of Financial Wisdom: Teach Yourself (and Your Kids) How to Live Wealthy with Little Money.* Deadwood: Wyatt-MacKenzie Publishing.

Gardner, David. 2002. *The Motley Fool Investment Guide for Teens: 8 Steps to Having More Money Than Your Parents Ever Dreamed Of.* New York: Fireside.

Grosz, Ornella. 2010. *Moneylicious: A Financial Clue for Generation Y.* Bloomington: Transformation Media Books.

Sember, Brette. 2008. *The Everything Kids' Money Book.* Avon: Adams Media.

WEB SITES

Annual Credit Report

https://www.annualcreditreport.com

Only site where you can request your FREE credit reports

Budget Diet

http://www.thebudgetdiet.com/

Tips for finding deals and saving money

Bureau of Engraving and Printing (BEP)

http://www.moneyfactory.gov/

The part of the U.S. Department of the Treasury that is responsible for designing and printing U.S. paper currency

Coupon Cabin

http://www.couponcabin.com/

Coupon codes, printable coupons, and free deals

Dollar Sensei

http://www.dollarsensei.com/TSAC/

Information on money management, debt, and college costs

eBay

http://www.ebay.com/

Make money by selling your items on this auction site

Equifax

www.equifax.com

Phone: 800-685-1111 (toll-free)

One of the three major credit bureaus

Etsy

http://www.etsy.com/

Earn extra cash by selling crafts and other homemade items

Experian

Phone: 888-397-3742 (toll-free)

www.experian.com

One of the three major credit bureaus

FAFSA

www.fafsa.ed.gov

Free Application for Federal Student Aid, which is required for any federal student aid

FatWallet

http://www.fatwallet.com/

Find out about hot deals, coupon codes, and "inside secrets" from bargain hunters

FinAid

http://www.finaid.org/

Comprehensive source of information and advice related to financial aid. The site also has links to a bunch of scholarship search sites

FTC Identity Theft Site

http://www.ftc.gov/idtheft

Get tips on protecting yourself from identity theft and what to do if you believe you've been a victim of identity theft

Garage Sale Gal

http://www.garagesalegal.com/

Tips and advice on finding great deals at garage sales—or hosting an awesome garage sale of your own

H&R Block Dollars and Sense

http://www.hrblockdollarsandsense.com/

Personal finance education for teens with a scholarship challenge where groups of teens from across the country can compete for several scholarships

Help Save My Dollars

http://helpsavemydollars.com/

Founded by a teenager, this site offers tips and resources to help you learn about money, save money, and find good deals on textbooks

Internal Revenue Service (IRS)

http://www.irs.gov/

This is the agency in charge of collecting federal taxes. Use the Web site to find out about tax forms you may need to complete, tax deductions, and how to fill out a tax return.

Mint.com

https://www.mint.com/

Find lots of cool money management and budgeting resources here, including tools that let you create colorful charts and graphs showing where your money goes.

PayDivvy

https://www.paydivvy.com

Allows you to pay a variety of bills online from one place and has a cool feature that helps split payments among groups of friends

Pinecone Research

http://www.pineconeresearch.com/

Get paid to take surveys or try out products

Practical Money Skills for Life

http://www.practicalmoneyskills.com/

Financial literacy tools, games, and information for teens, adults, and educators

TheMint.org

http://themint.org/

Sponsored by The Northwestern Mutual Foundation; lots of information and helpful tools on money-related topics, including fun stuff for kids.

TransUnion

Phone: 800-888-4213 (toll-free)

www.transunion.com

One of the three major credit bureaus

United States Mint

http://www.usmint.gov/

A government agency that produces and distributes coins, precious metals, and collectible coins

Utoria

www.myutoria.com

Site designed to help teenage girls learn about business and making money

WePay

www.wepay.com

Online e-commerce store page with easy setup

WOW! Zone

http://www.tdbank.com/wowzone/teens/

Sponsored by TD Bank; interactive tools to help teens learn about money, including budget worksheets

Printed in the USA
CPSIA information can be obtained
at www.ICGtesting.com
JSHW052016140824
68134JS00027B/2509